THE PHANTOM PUBLIC

Library of Conservative Thought

THE PHANTOM PUBLIC

WALTER LIPPMANN

With a New Introduction
by Wilfred M. McClay

Transaction Publishers
New Brunswick (U.S.A.) and London (U.K.)

Library of Congress Catalog Number: 92-41593
ISBN: 1-56000-677-3
Printed in the United States of America

Library of Congress Cataloging-in-Publication Data

Lippmann, Walter, 1889-1974
    The phantom public / Walter Lippmann ; with a new introduction by
Wilfred M. McClay
        p. cm.—(Library of conservative thought)
    Originally published: New York: Macmillan Co., 1927
    Includes bibliographical references and index.
    ISBN 1-56000-677-3
    1. Public opinion. 2. Political science. I. Title, II. Series

HM261.L74   1993
303.3'8—dc20   92-41593
                                                            CIP

TO
LEARNED HAND

"*The Voice of the People has been said to be the voice of God: and however generally this maxim has been quoted and believed, it is not true in fact.*"—Alexander Hamilton, June 18, 1787, at the Federal Convention (Yates's notes, cited *Sources and Documents Illustrating the American Revolution,* edited by S. G. Morison).

"*. . . consider 'Government by Public Opinion' as a formula. . . . It is an admirable formula: but it presupposes, not only that public opinion exists, but that on any particular question there is a public opinion ready to decide the issue. Indeed, it presupposes that the supreme statesman in democratic government is public opinion. Many of the shortcomings of democratic government are due to the fact that public opinion is not necessarily a great statesman at all.*"—From "Some Thoughts on Public Life," a lecture by Viscount Grey of Fallodon, February 3, 1923.

Contents

INTRODUCTION TO THE
TRANSACTION EDITION

IN THE nearly two decades since his death in 1974, Walter Lippmann and his works can hardly be said to have suffered an eclipse or a fall into obscurity. On the contrary; a fairly wide selection of that master journalist's book-length studies have continued in print, ranging from his early Progressive manifesto, *Drift and Mastery* (1914) and his critical understanding of the dilemmas of information dissemination in a modern democracy, *Public Opinion* (1922), to his later attempt to articulate and counteract the maladies of democracy in *The Public Philosophy* (1955), all readily available in inexpensive editions, still widely read and respected in a variety of fields. In addition, the publication of Ronald Steel's well-received 1980 biography of Lippmann and John Morton Blum's selection of Lippmann's correspondence have further stimulated and sus-

tained interest in Lippmann and his oeuvre,
as have the important and thoughtful recent
intellectual biographies of his contemporar-
ies Reinhold Niebuhr and John Dewey, with
whose careers Lippmann's intersected im-
portantly.[1]

Given such interest, Transaction's wel-
come decision to bring back into print many
of Lippmann's distinguished works reflects
a more general intellectual engagement
with his work that is not likely to slacken
anytime soon. Indeed, there is good reason
to think that Lippmann's work may come to
be seen as more, rather than less, important
and influential in the years to come. As
Americans continue to struggle with the
prospects and problems of their experiment
in mass democracy, Lippmann's fearless
criticism of modern American democracy
may serve as an increasingly valuable intellectual touchstone in contemporary debate,
where the disparaging term "elitist" has too
often served as the ultimate trump card and

conversation-stopper. Even if Francis Fukuyama is right in asserting that all the ideological alternatives to liberal democracy in our time have been exhausted—and that is surely a temporary state of affairs, at most—an awareness of the pathologies of democracy suggests a continuing need for frequent and sustained democratic self-criticism.[2] Although the gloomy and demythologized view of democracy found in *The Phantom Public* is hardly likely to convert mainstream public opinion—such a development being unlikely virtually by definition—it preserves a serious and distinctive intellectual option, one that is not without considerable sympathetic resonances and precursors in the American past. As the historian Daniel Walker Howe has pointed out, Lippmann may be seen in many respects as standing squarely in the intellectual tradition of the American Whigs.[3] And the first epigraph of *The Phantom Public*, which ridicules the adage *Vox populi, vox dei,* suggests

an even more influential intellectual pro-
venance: the antidemocratic skepticism of
Alexander Hamilton, and the antidemotic
fears of so many of the continental-minded
men who drafted and campaigned for the
U.S. Constitution.[4]

Such historical continuity is not in itself a
sufficient argument for Lippmann's importance. But the astonishing contemporary rel-
evance of much of his work is. Sentences and
paragraphs out of *The Phantom Public* could
be lifted, unchanged, out of their context and
be republished on the editorial pages of one
of today's great American newspapers,
where they might well win a Pulitzer for the
plagiarist intrepid enough to appropriate
them. (For instance, the book's first nine
pages, which comprise a chapter entitled
"The Disenchanted Man," can easily be
mined for observations that seem to speak
directly to the discontent, and non-voting
behavior, of the American electorate *circa*
1992.) Moreover, Lippmann's cool, analyti-

cal acuity and complete eschewal of moral posturing should forestall any dismissive charge against him of self-interested elitism, moss-backed crankishness, or crypto-legitimism. As those who have read *Public Opinion* can attest, Lippmann's discussion of stereotypes and propaganda in the modern mass-communications media, written at a time when radio was in its infancy and television little more than a pipedream, has hardly been improved upon by seven decades' worth of subsequent writers, a veritable army of scribblers which had the advantage of observing those media in full operation.

The Phantom Public is arguably an even more valuable text, precisely because it was perhaps the clearest, pithiest, and most full-throated expression of Lippmann's crystallizing skepticism. Perhaps it was for that very reason that *The Phantom Public* disappeared from print so rapidly, and has remained so until now. Though it was acceptable, and even amusing, for a semicomic literary virtuoso like H.L. Mencken to mouth disdain for democracy and public opinion, such opinions were quite another matter coming from a man of Lippmann's reputed probity and wide influence. Lippmann himself came to suspect, before publication, that an untoward fate might lie in store for the book. Although he had written it as a shorter and more popularly aimed sequel to *Public Opinion*, which had enjoyed considerable intellectual and popular success, Lippmann worried that the more pointed and damning argument of *The Phantom Public* would get him in trouble, and even see him "put on trial for heresy by my old friends on *The New Republic*."[5]

Few of these immediate apprehensions were realized. True, a handful of the book's reviewers suggested that Lippmann had indeed transgressed the limits of acceptable sentiment. The New York *Times*'s reviewer claimed Lippmann's "sweeping indictment" had caused him to "overstate his case"; and the *New Statesman* casually dismissed the book as "disappointing."[6] But such reviews were hardly the norm, and it is therefore hard to credit Ronald Steel's characterization of *The Phantom Public*'s reception as overwhelmingly negative (though his assessment of the book's virtues seems more on target):

> The [book's] argument, for all its bleakness, deserved a better hearing than it got. ... [M]ost reviewers were disheartened by its seeming pessimism. *The Phantom Public* soon went out of print, and in the years since has been virtually forgotten. This neglect is unfortunate, for it is one of Lippmann's most powerfully argued and revealing books. In it he came fully to terms with the inadequacy of traditional democratic theory.[7]

Indeed, no better testimony to the power and importance of *The Phantom Public* can be found than the seriousness and admiration with which it *was* read (and reviewed in the pages of the *New Republic*) by John Dewey, who was so stimulated by it that he went on to write one of his most ringing and durable defenses of democracy, *The Public and Its Problems* (1927), as an attempt at rebuttal.[8]

As it turns out, many of the contemporary reviews of *The Phantom Public* were unqualified raves, quite as favorable as Steel's retrospective one. Harold Lasswell enthused over its "cogent and spirited qualities." Another reviewer called it "a champion's performance" by a "dynamiter of fallacious doctrines of government and exploder of specious political arguments." Yet another proclaimed that

The Phantom Public, like *Public Opinion*, will become one of the modern classics of American political thought. And it is a book that will be read and reread for pure delight in its rare literary quality.

The influential Senator William E. Borah, writing in the New York *World*, went so far as to call it "one of those rare books which startles one into a realization of how stupendous is the task before us as a people if we are to carry to a successful conclusion the work initiated in 1789."[9] Given this degree of favorable reception, the mystery of *The Phantom Public*'s phantom-like disappearance from public sight seems even harder to fathom. Perhaps the only plausible answer is the most obvious one: that the challenges it poses, and the implications of those challenges for the conduct of practical politics, have proved too unpleasant or difficult for even its most ardent admirers—or at any rate those less well-equipped than John Dewey—to face in a sustained manner.

It is not coincidental, then, that the debate with Dewey provides us a useful point of departure in exploring Lippmann's aims in writing *The Phantom Public*. No concept, after all, had been more central to the Progressive vision of social reform than that of "the public"; the efforts to tame special interests which so often animated Progressive reform were always undertaken in the name of "the public interest," and it was generally assumed that such a thing as the "public" existed, and that its "interest" could be ascertained. Indeed, the term "disinterested," which is, significantly, so frequently misunderstood and misused in our own time, carried a powerfully ethical, indeed almost religious, weight in Progressive social thought—for no word was freighted with greater negative import in the vocabulary of Progressivism than the noun "Interests." A favorite term of abuse for muckraking journalists, "the Interests" not only stood for the specific venality of Standard Oil and the other "trusts," or for other self-interested groups. In a deeper sense it came to stand for the pernicious values of individualism, particularism, self-seeking, and growing social inequality: for everything that threatened to corrupt the great American experiment in political democracy.[10]

"Disinterestedness" stood for a contrasting vision of hope, of common subjection to the rule of the common good: an unsullied ideal of theoretical and practical expertise, to be administered conscientiously, impartially, and selflessly by an enlightened "new middle class" trained in the burgeoning new research universities. In such places, this new knowledge class would be versed in the scientific and action-oriented knowledge needed to produce a just and rationally ordered public realm. Such a new middle class would not be imprisoned by the shortsighted pursuit of self-interest, or the false individualism of classical-liberal economics; it would instead be bound by the self-regulating and rational autonomy of professional organizations, and the uncorrupted social altruism of those trained to identify the public interest and pursue the common weal.

The ideal of science was no less crucial to Lippmann than to Dewey. But Dewey trusted that the inherent democracy of science—since science was by its very nature no respecter of persons or of untestable sources of authority—would make it eminently compatible with democracy; indeed, the *only* form of authority ultimately so compatible.[11] The key link between science and democracy in the Deweyan scheme was the concept of the "public" as an ideal point of convergence and interaction. Without the distinctive assumption of a "public interest," which could be articulated through institutions of political democracy and clarified through the disinterested resources of scientific intelligence, the essential moral core of the Progressive strain of political and social thought would collapse. There had to be something called a *public*, and it had to have an identifiable *interest*, distinguishable from that of any of its constituent elements. Social science not only possessed the capacity to reveal that interest, but the authority to show the citizen how the public interest was also his own.

Lippmann had held to such views when a younger man. No one had written a more eloquent brief for the scientific ideal as a basis for cultural authority in a post-religious democratic era than Lippmann's *Drift and Mastery* (1914), a book whose title nouns became transformed into bywords for the stark dilemmas facing the era.[12] But Lippmann's restless intelligence, always alert to the flow of events, had quickly moved beyond the confines of its youthful productions. And in the wake of the First World War's many disappointments for Progressives, particularly the Wilson Administration's heavyhanded use of domestic propaganda and curtailment of civil liberties to impose univocal public support for the war effort, his view of democratic governance and its connection with the ethos of science changed dramatically. In *Public Opinion* he argued that, because citizens in a modern mass democracy made decisions strictly on the basis of media-generated stereotypes, experts would have to be brought into the process, to control and adjust the flow of information to the public in order to keep the "pictures in their heads" in line with realities that only an expert few could properly understand.[13] The domestic wartime propaganda emanating from the Creel Committee had taught Lippmann how frighteningly plastic and manipulable public opinion was. The only sensible solution to the problem was to attempt to assert rational mastery over it.

But by 1925 Lippmann's doubts had deepened considerably. The opening pages of *The Phantom Public* even echo some of the quintessential gestures of Twenties postwar intellectual disillusionment, à la Hemingway and Fitzgerald. He depicted the un-illusioned reconsiderations of the "disenchanted man" in terms so vivid that it seems likely that he was in part describing himself, and declaring his own somewhat jaundiced "farewell to reform":

> For when the private man has lived through the romantic age in politics and is no longer moved by the stale echoes of its hot cries, when he is sober and unimpressed, his own part in public affairs appears to him a pretentious thing, a second rate, an inconsequential. You cannot move him then with a good straight talk about service and civic duty, nor by waving a flag in his face, nor by sending a boy scout after him to make him vote. He is a man back home from a crusade to make the world something or other it did not become; he has been tantalized too often by the foam of events, has seen the gas go out of it.[14]

But more than his mood had changed in *The Phantom Public*; so too had his substantive concerns about the limitations of democracy. Not only was it inconceivable to him that the average voter was capable of governance—such being the untenable democratic myth of what Lippmann called "the sovereign and omnicompetent citizen"—but it now seemed to him that there was really no such thing as the public.[15] What was called the public was merely a "phantom"; to the extent that there was a genuine and effective public, it was to be defined *ad hoc*, situationally and operationally, simply as "those persons who are interested in an affair." As for the grand claims of expertise, on whose behalf Lippmann had formerly spoken with such conviction, these too began to be severely circumscribed; the important distinction was not that between experts and amateurs, but that between "insiders" and "outsiders," those with firsthand knowledge in a *particular* affair or circumstance, and those without such knowledge.

Lippmann's assault was directed, both here and in *Public Opinion*, towards more than mere naive democratic sentimentalism. It was addressed to the very core of Progressive politics, and by extension to any conception of politics that was holistic and systemic, that spoke in the false terminology of a "body politic," and sought to coordinate political decision-making according to a model of an operating whole. In this new post-Progressive realist and pluralist dispensation, men were

> denied the fraudulent support of the fiction that they are agents of a common purpose. They are regarded as agents of special purposes, without pretense and without embarrassment. They must live in a world with men who have other special purposes. The adjustments which must be made *are* society. . . . When men take a position in respect to the purposes of others they are acting as a public.[16]

Generally, the central problem for decision-making in a democratic society had been understood as that of finding a way to keep the citizenry informed, so that they could correctly assess and address the issues facing a complex and interconnected modern society. But Lippmann held out little hope for this standard bromide of civics textbooks; any such "appeal to education as the remedy for the incompetence of democracy," he asserted, is "barren."[17] The Poloniuses who authored such tomes seemed unaware that even under the best of conditions, "the citizen gives but a little of his time to public affairs, has but a casual interest in facts and but a poor appetite for theory." And the eager-beaver citizen who attempts earnestly to look to all his prescribed duties, from the upkeep of a subway in Brooklyn to the rights of Britain in the Sudan, will end up "as bewildered as a puppy trying to lick three bones at once," for he "cannot know all about everything all the time, and while he is watching one thing a thousand others undergo great changes."[18] Such omnicompetence was an unattainable ideal, the "mystical fallacy of democracy," and a false, pernicious, and disenchanting one at that.[19]

Had he taken a position no further than this, Lippmann might well have earned dismissal as an elitist. But he had a good deal more to say. If the common man was not, *contra* the American democratic tradition from Jefferson to Bryan, a font of untutored wisdom competent to decide all things, or at least educable to that station, then neither, Lippmann asserted, was the expert. The modern interconnected world, the Great Society, was far too complex to be comprehended by anyone, even by experts.[20] For expertise was only authoritative in relation to some particular subject or task—and no more. Efforts at a comprehensive understanding of, and coordination of, polity and economy could never move much beyond the condition of the proverbial blind men examining the elephant; their local and special knowledge could not be reliably extrapolated or transferred to a comprehensive map, a structural whole. "The work of the world is carried on," he explained,

> by men in their executive capacity, by an infinite number of concrete acts, plowing and planting and reaping, building and destroying, fitting this to that, going from here to there, transforming A into B and moving B from X to Y.

Such work is regulated by "a most intricate mechanism of exchange, of contract, of custom and of implied promises," all of them highly *particular* in nature. To allow any single authority to attempt the governance of all these matters was extremely ill-advised.

But to turn such authority over to *public opinion* was an even worse mistake, ensuring either abject failure or complete tyranny.[21] There was a simple reason for this: the sovereignty of the people was a pure fiction. Standard democratic theory refused to recognize that "the functioning of government" was distinct from "the will of the people." The latter is itself merely a reification of the particular decisions that, for prudential reasons of orderly governance, needed to be put to the people collectively for adjudication. The public does not, properly speaking, *express* its opinion; it merely *aligns* itself for or against a person or proposition. The people do not govern; they merely "support or oppose the individuals who actually govern." The "popular will" only intervenes occasionally, to counteract willful and arbitrary force through its alignment choices.

The principal positive use of public opinion then, he believed, was in times of crisis—a reflection which suggests how fundamentally conservative were his expectations for public opinion's radically stripped-down role. Public opinion would "align men during the crisis of a problem in such a way as to favor the action of those individuals who may be able to compose the crisis."[22] Clearly,

abstract questions of justice, legitimacy, ultimate values, and so on, did not figure into
this formula in the slightest; it was an equi-
librist vision of a polity composed of count-
less competing pieces, and the purpose of
governance was to sustain the highest possible level of order and peace. Order and
legitimacy were virtually exchangable
terms. Public opinion was useful merely as
a final court of appeal, useful at those times
when government exhausted its ability to
resolve a conflict and avert ongoing social or
political discord. (Even an election, Lippmann asserted, was nothing more than a
sublimated form of civil war, its
majoritarianism a close cousin to the use of
brute force.) The *telos* of modern politics is
the achievement of a workable *modus vivendi* among competitive interests, since
premodern (and Progressive) notions of a
bridge between man's environment and his
(limited) political capacity no longer seem
tenable.[23] Lippmann instead posited a "deep

pluralism" as the inescapable condition placed upon all future modern political and economic speculation.[24] The political thinker, he declared, should "no longer expect to find a unity which absorbs diversity," but instead, rather than "looking for identity of purposes" should settle for "an accommodation of purposes."[25]

Such contentions show how fully Lippmann participated in the demystifying antiformalism of the generation of Charles Beard, Oliver Wendell Holmes, Thorstein Veblen, and John Dewey.[26] His notions of rights and duties, for example, were Holmesian and "realistic": a right was "a promise that a certain kind of behavior will be backed by the organized force of the state"; a duty was "a promise that failure to respect the rights of others in a certain way will be punished." Persistent beliefs that these things needed grounding in nature or divine fiat were little more than "tiresome illusions."[27] But Lippmann pressed his anti-

formalist convictions into new territory, pry-
ing the individual away from his social ma-
trix. By mercilessly smashing the unitary
Progressive notion of "the public" into its
multivalent constituent elements, Lippmann opened the way to a post-Progressive
conception of politics as a "realistic" process
of brokering an openly interest-based pluralism, a politics with no higher conception of
the public interest than, as in the subtitle of
Harold Lasswell's 1936 book *Politics*, "who
gets what, when, and how"—or E.E.
Schattschneider's dry observation that public policy was merely "the result of 'effective
demands' upon the government," or Thurman Arnold's jaded conclusion that public
debate over matters of political principle or
value was little more than the play of useful
mythologies and "magic words."[28]

Dewey meant *The Public and Its Problems*
as a direct and respectful attempt to answer
Lippmann's mounting pessimism (and
growing influence), and defend the demo-

cratic promise that was at the heart of American civil religion.[29] It valiantly held to the belief that the public was no phantom, but something quite real, though currently "in eclipse." The chief problems of "the public" revolved around the current lack of shared symbols ("intellectual instrumentalities for the formation of an organized public," in Deweyese) and inadequate communication of the "numerous, tough and subtle" bonds "which hold men together in action," whether or not they are fully conscious of it. Without them, he conceded, "the public will remain shadowy and formless, seeking spasmodically for itself, but seizing and holding its shadow rather than its substance." Until "the Great Society is converted into a Great Community," wrote Dewey, "the Public will remain in eclipse."[30] Such a response to Lippmann's skepticism, however, was far too abstract, even oddly idealistic in diction, to dispose of the problem. In the same year, Lippmann would write that "the more or less unconscious and unplanned activities of businessmen are for once more novel, more daring and in a sense more revolutionary, than the theories of the progressives."[31] Few more deliberately insulting rebukes to Deweyan intelligence, or more defiant apostasies from the faith of Herbert Croly and *The New Republic*, could be imagined.

The process begun in *The Phantom Public* continued to unfold for the remainder of the decade. By 1929, Lippmann's post-Progressive reaction had deepened even further, and borne fruit in his *Preface to Morals* (1929), which became a best-seller and Book-of-the-Month Club selection. That magisterial work echoed and restated the great theme Lippmann had been building upon for a decade and a half: the erosion of traditional forms of authority by the "acids of modernity," and the difficulty of finding substitutes for them. Even the cultural authority of science, so central to Dewey, had been called into question for Lippmann:

partly by the relativism of Einsteinian physics (Darwinism, which had been the source of Dewey's fundamental philosophical method, was now, Lippmann asserted, "outmoded"), which presented man with a bewildering physical universe wholly incommensurable with his inner life; and partly through a growing awareness of science's inherent limitations.[32]

On the latter point, Lippmann began with Charles Peirce's work on the social construction of scientific truth, and then went on to draw the devastating conclusion, training the antiformalist armory on science itself: "When we say that something has been 'explained' by science, we really mean only that our own curiosity is satisfied." As it advances, we see that scientific explanation "does not yield a certain picture of anything which can be taken naively as a representation of reality," but only "provisional dramatizations which are soon dissolved by the progress of science itself." Science was little more than a bag of elaborated and disciplined metaphors, applied variously to an ungraspable reality. Therefore, he concluded, a religion of "scientific materialism has nothing in it, except the pretension that it is a true account of the world"; scientific explanations "cannot give men such a clue to the plan of existence as they find in popular religion."[33] A prolegomenon to morals could begin by ruling out any scientific discovery and testing of moral principles. Science, in a word, could not tell us how to live.

All that was left, believed Lippmann, with all other supports teetering, was a highly ascetic understanding of the principle of "disinterestedness" itself, attached to a doctrine of "humanism" arising out of the phenomenology of human life, and directed towards the purification and discipline of the individual will.[34] The "ideal of disinterestedness," he asserted, is "inevitable in the modern world"; for only it can "untangle the moral confusion of the age." Disinterestedness in fact was the still-living "core of high religion," the "central insight of the teachers of wisdom" such as Jesus, Buddha, and Confucius.

Such disinterestedness was still present in science; indeed, "pure science is high religion incarnate," and one of the greatest services of science was its value as a school of disinterestedness, which "matures the human character" and teaches us not to regard "our desires, tastes, and interests as affording a key to the understanding of the world."[35] The modern world had seemed to teach men that emancipation from the old authorities meant they could at last pursue their passions without restraint, and thereby achieve happiness. But the lesson Lippmann drew was very different: we needed to learn to detach ourselves, not only from the tyranny of "public opinion," but from the force of our own desires.

Disinterestedness, detachment, asceticism, discipline, and disillusion; such then

were the guiding spirits of the *Preface*. Lippmann had indeed come a long way, by the
end of the twenties, from his days as a
habitué of Mabel Dodge's Greenwich Village
salon, an editor of Herbert Croly's *New Republic*, an apostle of progressive Mastery,
and a believer in the malleability of human
nature. Indeed, Lippmann's ascetic ideal
sounded more reminiscent of Nietzsche's
Zarathustra than of Progressive reformers
like Croly, who had also placed great stress
upon the value of disinterestedness.[36] But
Lippmann's disinterestedness now sub-
served a severely individual (and frankly
elitist) worldview; it was "a mountain track
which the many are likely in the future as
in the past to find cold, bleak, and bare." The
ideal man must "take the world as it comes,
and within himself remain quite unper-
turbed. . . . He would face pain with forti-
tude, for he would have put it away from the
inner chambers of his soul. Fear would not
haunt him."[37]

Such heroic accents contrasted strikingly with the anti-individualist, self-sacrificial, corporative ethos that writers from Edward Bellamy to Richard Ely to John Dewey had hoped a standard of the "public interest" might promote.[38] Not that notions of the public interest or of a consolidated and unified national community suddenly expired. They lived on and comprised one of the intellectual strains in the tangled history of the New Deal, visible, for example, in the efforts of the National Recovery Administration, or in the Civilian Conservation Corps, or in President Franklin Roosevelt's frequent invocation of the analogue of warfare—the ultimate unifying, self-transcending clarion call.[39] Such thoughts have continued to appear regularly in the rhetoric of American politicians; one thinks, for example, of President Jimmy Carter's 1979 "crisis of confidence" speech, in which he warned that the nation had embraced "a mistaken idea of freedom" and was heading down the path of "fragmentation and self-interest." Carter urged that Americans instead "rebuild the unity and confidence of America," because only by following the "path of common purpose" could we come into an experience of "true freedom."[40]

Yet it is perhaps an unanticipated legacy of works like *The Phantom Public*, and more generally of the "realist" approach to political analysis it exemplified and pioneered, that such appeals to common purpose have fallen increasingly upon deaf ears in this century, as Carter's case so conspicuously demonstrated. In a society that has increasingly come to embrace deep pluralism as normative, and instinctively suspects any appeal to founding principles, common culture, and common purpose as a snare set by would-be hegemonists, Lippmann's tough-minded and unsparing analysis of the vagaries of the concept of the "public" seem all too familiar and comfortable, even if one suspects that Lippmann would probably never have extended it quite so far as we have. In that connection, it is perhaps revealing to note that Lippmann himself changed intellectual course dramatically with the approach of the Second World War, breaking ranks with his erstwhile realist allies and embracing, in *The Good Society* (1937) and later *The Public Philosophy* (1955), the notion of a "higher" natural law as a bulwark of public morality. Like his contemporary Reinhold Niebuhr, Lippmann came to feel that belief in the purely social and instrumental sources of truth and justice provided no protection against the evil tendencies of human groups, and no firewall of defense against the rise of would-be *Übermenschen* like Hitler.[41]

But whatever else may be said about this shift, it did not represent much of a change in Lippmann's view of democracy. One of the principal uses of a higher law, in his view, was precisely as a brake against the rash actions of popular majorities, such as those that allowed Hitler to come to power. Lippmann was willing to adapt and even sacrifice many of his cherished beliefs in the course of his life. But his skeptical view of popular democracy was not one of them. Such stubborn "elitism" may be precisely why we ought to continue to read him in the years to come. In an era pervasively disgusted with politicians, and entranced by public-opinion polling, initiatives, referenda, and the interactive gadgetry of "direct democracy," the fundamental contention at the core of *The Phantom Public* remains as stubbornly and painfully relevant as ever: that "public opinion" does not, and simply cannot, rule a nation or propound its policy, but may merely choose between alternatives propounded and proposed by competing elites. Advocates of direct democracy, and the disgruntled American electorate, would do well to ponder that assertion, even if they disagree with it in the end.

Wilfred M. McClay

Notes

[1] Ronald Steel, *Walter Lippmann and the American Century* (Boston, 1980); John Morton Blum, ed. *Public Philosopher: Selected Letters of Walter Lippmann* (New York, 1985); Richard Wightman Fox, *Reinhold Niebuhr: A Biography* (New York, 1985); Robert B. Westbrook, *John Dewey and American Democracy* (Ithaca, 1991); and Steven C. Rockefeller, *John Dewey: Religious Faith and Democratic Humanism* (New York, 1991).

[2] Fukuyama's book *The End of History and the Last Man* (New York, 1992) is itself an effort in precisely such democratic self-criticism.

[3] Daniel Walker Howe, *The Political Culture of the American Whigs* (Chicago, 1979), 304.

[4] For the debate animating the Constitutionalists, see Gordon S. Wood, *The Creation of the American Republic, 1776–1787* (Chapel Hill, 1969), 469–615; on Hamilton see Forrest McDonald, *Alexander Hamilton: A Biography* (New York, 1979).

[5] Steel, *Walter Lippmann*, 212.

[6] See New York *Times*, October 25, 1925; *New Statesman*, November 14, 1925.

[7] Steel, *Walter Lippmann*, 214.

[8] Dewey directly acknowledges the influence of *The Phantom Public* in the text of *The Public and Its Problems* (New York, 1927), 116–17.

[9] Lasswell's review was in the *American Journal of Sociology* 31 (January 1926), 533; others appeared in *Literary Review*, February 27, 1926, 5; *Springfield Republican*, November 15, 1925, 7; and New York *World*, November 8, 1925, 6.

[10] The superb chapter entitled "Interests," in Daniel Rodgers, *Contested Truths: Keywords in American Politics Since Independence* (New York, 1987), 176–211.

[11] See James Kloppenberg, *Uncertain Victory: Social Democracy and Progressivism in European and American Thought, 1870–1920* (New York, 1986), offers an excellent discussion of these matters; see especially 384.

[12] David Hollinger, "Science and Anarchy: Walter Lippmann's *Drift and Mastery*" in *In the American Province: Studies in the History and Historiography of Ideas* (Baltimore, 1989), 44–55.

[13] Walter Lippmann, *Public Opinion* (New York, 1922).

[14] Walter Lippmann, *The Phantom Public* (New York, 1925), 15.

[15] Ibid., 21.

[16] Ibid., 198 (my emphasis).

[17] Ibid., 26.

[18] Ibid., 24–25.

[19] Ibid., 38–39.

[20] Lippmann's (and Dewey's) use of the term "Great Society" should not be confused with the term's subsequent use by American President Lyndon B. Johnson. Lippmann derived the term from a book of the same name by his friend Graham Wallas, which argued for the inevitable interconnectedness of modern technological and commercial society, and the ravaged impotence of earlier forms of *Gemeinschaften*, small-scale, premodern forms of association. As such, the term here has none of the moral grandeur Johnson imputed to it.

[21] Lippmann, *The Phantom Public*, 70–71.

[22] Ibid., 68.

[23] Ibid., 78–79.

[24] Ibid., 97.

[25] Ibid., 98.

[26] The term initially comes from one of Dewey's partisans, Morton White, in his *Social Thought in America: The Revolt Against Formalism* (Boston, 1949), but the term "antiformalist" has recently come to be used both with greater precision and more powerful suggestiveness in a variety of works by the historian Thomas Haskell.

[27] Lippmann, *The Phantom Public*, 100–01.

[28] Harold D. Lasswell, *Politics: Who Gets What, When, How* (New York, 1936); E. E. Schattschneider, *Politics, Pressures and the Tariff: A Study of Free Private Enterprise in Pressure Politics* (New York, 1935); Thurman Arnold, *The Folklore of Capitalism* (New Haven, 1937); and *The Symbols of Government* (New Haven, 1935); Charles Merriam, *Political Power* (New York, 1934). For a helpful overview discussion of this development in political science,

see Edward A. Purcell, Jr., *The Crisis of Democratic Theory: Scientific Naturalism and the Problem of Value* (Lexington, KY, 1973), esp. 95–114.

[29] Robert N. Bellah, "Civil Religion in America," *Daedalus* 96 (Winter 1967), 1–21, is the classic text on this subject, though one should also consult his later work *The Broken Covenant* (New York, 1975), and the work of his student Robert Wuthnow, particularly *The Restructuring of American Religion: Society and Faith Since World War II* (Princeton, 1988), 242–57, 283–96. It is extremely relevant to note that Bellah's most recent work, his collaborative study *The Good Society* (New York, 1991), which is a sequel to the enormously successful collaborative book *Habits of the Heart* (Berkeley, 1985), relies explicitly and extensively upon *The Public and Its Problems* in making a case for a revivified public realm (and transcendence of interest-group politics) in contemporary American life.

[30] Dewey, *The Public and Its Problems*, 142.

[31] Walter Lippmann, *Men of Destiny* (New York, 1927), 228.

[32] On Darwinism, see Walter Lippmann to Newton D. Baker, May 15, 1929, in John Morton Blum, ed. *Public Philosopher: Selected Letters of Walter Lippmann* (New York, 1985), 240–41.

[33] Walter Lippmann, *A Preface to Morals* (New York, 1929), 130–31.

[34] Ibid., 193–95; see also Lippmann to Baker in Blum, ed., *Public Philosopher*, 240–41.

[35] Lippmann, *Preface to Morals*, 238–39, 311–13, 326–28.

[36] Herbert Croly, *The Promise of American Life* (New York, 1090), esp. 409–12.

[37] Lippmann, *Preface to Morals*, 313, 329.

[38] For a discussion of this tendency see R. Jackson Wilson, *In Quest of Community: Social Philosophy in the United States, 1860–1920* (New York, 1968).

[39] Ellis Hawley, *The New Deal and the Problem of Monopoly: A Study in Economic Ambivalence* (Princeton, 1966); Eric Gorham, "The Ambiguous Practices of the Civilian Conservation Corps," *Social History* 17 (May 1992), 229–49 William Leuchtenburg, "The New Deal and the Analogue of War," in John Braeman, Robert

Bremner and Everett Walters, eds., *Change and Continuity in Twentieth-Century America* (Columbus, 1964), 81–143.

[40] New York *Times*, July 16, 1979, A10.

[41] Reinhold Niebuhr, *Moral Man and Immoral Society* (New York, 1932), was the classic expression of this concern from Niebuhr's theological (or quasi-theological) perspective.

PART I

Chapter I

THE DISENCHANTED MAN

I

THE private citizen today has come to feel rather like a deaf spectator in the back row, who ought to keep his mind on the mystery off there, but cannot quite manage to keep awake. He knows he is somehow affected by what is going on. Rules and regulations continually, taxes annually and wars occasionally remind him that he is being swept along by great drifts of circumstance.

Yet these public affairs are in no convincing way his affairs. They are for the most part invisible. They are managed, if they are managed at all, at distant centers, from behind the scenes, by unnamed powers. As a private person he does not know for certain what is going on, or who is doing it, or where he is being carried. No newspaper reports his

environment so that he can grasp it; no school
has taught him how to imagine it; his ideals,
often, do not fit with it; listening to speeches,
uttering opinions and voting do not, he
finds, enable him to govern it. He lives in
a world which he cannot see, does not understand and is unable to direct.

In the cold light of experience he knows
that his sovereignty is a fiction. He reigns
in theory, but in fact he does not govern.
Contemplating himself and his actual accom-
plishments in public affairs, contrasting the
influence he exerts with the influence he is
supposed according to democratic theory to
exert, he must say of his sovereignty what
Bismarck said of Napoleon III.: "At a distance it is something, but close to it is nothing at all." [1] When, during an agitation of
some sort, say a political campaign, he hears
himself and some thirty million others described as the source of all wisdom and power
and righteousness, the prime mover and the

[1] Cited Philip Guedalla, *The Second Empire.*

ultimate goal, the remnants of sanity in him protest. He cannot all the time play Chanticleer who was so dazzled and delighted because he himself had caused the sun to rise.

For when the private man has lived through the romantic age in politics and is no longer moved by the stale echoes of its hot cries, when he is sober and unimpressed, his own part in public affairs appears to him a pretentious thing, a second rate, an inconsequential. You cannot move him then with a good straight talk about service and civic duty, nor by waving a flag in his face, nor by sending a boy scout after him to make him vote. He is a man back home from a crusade to make the world something or other it did not become; he has been tantalized too often by the foam of events, has seen the gas go out of it, and, with sour derision for the stuff, he is saying with the author of *Trivia:* [2]

"'Self-determination,' one of them insisted.

[2] Logan Pearsall Smith, *More Trivia*, p. 41.

"'Arbitration,' cried another.

"'Coöperation,' suggested the mildest of the party.

"'Confiscation,' answered an uncompromising female.

"I, too, became intoxicated with the sound of these vocables. And were they not the cure for all our ills?

"'Inoculation!' I chimed in. 'Transubstantiation, alliteration, inundation, flagellation, and afforestation!'"

2

It is well known that nothing like the whole people takes part in public affairs. Of the eligible voters in the United States less than half go to the polls even in a presidential year.[3] During the campaign of 1924 a special effort

[3] *Cf.* Simon Michelet, *Stay-at-Home Vote and Absentee Voters,* pamphlet of the National Get Out the Vote Club; also A. M. Schlesinger and E. M. Erickson, "The Vanishing Voter," *New Republic,* Oct. 15, 1924. The percentage of the popular to the eligible vote from 1865 to 1920 declined from 83.51 per cent to 52.36 per cent.

was made to bring out more voters. They did not come out. The Constitution, the nation, the party system, the presidential succession, private property, all were supposed to be in danger. One party prophesied red ruin, another black corruption, a third tyranny and imperialism if the voters did not go to the polls in greater numbers. Half the citizenship was unmoved.

The students used to write books about voting. They are now beginning to write books about nonvoting. At the University of Chicago Professor Merriam and Mr. Gosnell have made an elaborate inquiry [4] into the reason why, at the typical Chicago mayoral election of 1923, there were, out of 1,400,000 eligible electors, only 900,000 who registered, and out of those who registered there were only 723,000 who finally managed to vote. Thousands of persons were interviewed. About 30 per cent of the abstainers had,

[4] Charles Edward Merriam and Harvey Foote Gosnell, *Non-Voting: Causes and Methods of Control.*

or at least claimed to have had, an insuperable difficulty about going to the polls. They were ill, they were absent from the city, they were women detained at home by a child or an invalid, they had had insufficient legal residence. The other 70 per cent, representing about half a million free and sovereign citizens of this Republic, did not even pretend to have a reason for not voting, which, in effect, was not an admission that they did not care about voting. They were needed at their work, the polls were crowded, the polls were inconveniently located, they were afraid to tell their age, they did not believe in woman suffrage, the husband objected, politics is rotten, elections are rotten, they were afraid to vote, they did not know there was an election. About a quarter of those who were interviewed had the honesty to say they were wholly uninterested.

Yet Bryce is authority for the statement that "the will of the sovereign people is expressed . . . in the United States . . . by as large a proportion of the registered voters as in any other country." [5] And certainly Mr. Lowell's tables on the use of the initiative and referendum in Switzerland in the main support the view that the indifference of the American voter is not unique.[6] In fact, realistic political thinkers in Europe long ago abandoned the notion that the collective mass of the people direct the course of public affairs. Robert Michels, himself a Socialist, says flatly that "the majority is permanently incapable of self-government," [7] and quotes approvingly the remark of a Swedish Socialist Deputy, Gustaf F. Steffen, that "even after the victory there will always remain in political life the leaders and the led." Michels, who is a political thinker of great penetration, unburdens himself finally on the subject by printing a remark of Hertzen's

[5] James Bryce, *Modern Democracies*, Vol. II, p. 52.

[6] A. Lawrence Lowell, *Public Opinion and Popular Government.* *Cf.* Appendices.

[7] Robert Michels, *Political Parties*, p. 390.

that the victory of an opposition party amounts to "passing from the sphere of envy to the sphere of avarice."

There is then nothing particularly new in the disenchantment which the private citizen expresses by not voting at all, by voting only for the head of the ticket, by staying away from the primaries, by not reading speeches and documents, by the whole list of sins of omission for which he is denounced. I shall not denounce him further. My sympathies are with him, for I believe that he has been saddled with an impossible task and that he is asked to practice an unattainable ideal. I find it so myself for, although public business is my main interest and I give most of my time to watching it, I cannot find time to do what is expected of me in the theory of democracy; that is, to know what is going on and to have an opinion worth expressing on every question which confronts a self-governing community. And I have not happened to meet anybody, from a President of the United States to a professor of political science, who came anywhere near to embodying the accepted ideal of the sovereign and omnicompetent citizen.

Chapter II

THE UNATTAINABLE IDEAL

I HAVE tried to imagine how the perfect citizen could be produced. Some say he will have to be born of the conjunction of the right germ plasms, and, in the pages of books written by Madison Grant, Lothrop Stoddard and other revivalists, I have seen prescriptions as to just who ought to marry whom to produce a great citizenry. Not being a biologist I keep an open but hopeful mind on this point, tempered, however, with the knowledge that certainty about how to breed ability in human beings is on the whole in inverse proportion to the writer's scientific reputation.

It is then to education that logically one turns next, for education has furnished the thesis of the last chapter of every optimistic book on democracy written for one hundred and fifty years. Even Robert Michels, stern

12

and unbending antisentimentalist that he is, says in his "final considerations" that "it is the great task of social education to raise the intellectual level of the masses, so that they may be enabled, within the limits of what is possible, to counteract the oligarchical tendencies" of all collective action.

So I have been reading some of the new standard textbooks used to teach citizenship in schools and colleges. After reading them I do not see how any one can escape the conclusion that man must have the appetite of an encyclopædist and infinite time ahead of him. To be sure he no longer is expected to remember the exact salary of the county clerk and the length of the coroner's term. In the new civics he studies the problems of government, and not the structural detail. He is told, in one textbook of five hundred concise, contentious pages, which I have been reading, about city problems, state problems, national problems, international problems, trust problems, labor problems, transportation problems, banking problems, rural problems, agricultural problems, and so on *ad infinitum*. In the eleven pages devoted to problems of the city there are described twelve sub-problems.

But nowhere in this well-meant book is the sovereign citizen of the future given a hint as to how, while he is earning a living, rearing children and enjoying his life, he is to keep himself informed about the progress of this swarming confusion of problems. He is exhorted to conserve the natural resources of the country because they are limited in quantity. He is advised to watch public expenditures because the taxpayers cannot pay out indefinitely increasing amounts. But he, the voter, the citizen, the sovereign, is apparently expected to yield an unlimited quantity of public spirit, interest, curiosity and effort. The author of the textbook, touching on everything, as he thinks, from city sewers to Indian opium, misses a decisive fact: the citizen gives but a little of his time to public affairs, has but a casual interest in facts and but a poor appetite for theory.

It never occurs to this preceptor of civic duty to provide the student with a rule by which he can know whether on Thursday it is his duty to consider subways in Brooklyn or the Manchurian Railway, nor how, if he determines on Thursday to express his sovereign will on the subway question, he is to repair those gaps in his knowledge of that question which are due to his having been preoccupied the day before in expressing his sovereign will about rural credits in Montana and the rights of Britain in the Sudan. Yet he cannot know all about everything all the time, and while he is watching one thing a thousand others undergo great changes. Unless he can discover some rational ground for fixing his attention where it will do the most good, and in a way that suits his inherently amateurish equipment, he will be as bewildered as a puppy trying to lick three bones at once.

I do not wish to say that it does the student no good to be taken on a sightseeing tour of the problems of the world. It may teach him that the world is complicated, even if he comes out of the adventure "laden with germs, breathing creeds and convictions on you whenever he opens his mouth." [1] He may learn humility, but most certainly his acquaintance with what a high-minded author thought were American problems in 1925 will not equip him to master American problems ten years later. Unless out of the study of transient issues he acquires an intellectual attitude no education has occurred.

That is why the usual appeal to education as the remedy for the incompetence of democracy is so barren. It is, in effect, a proposal that school teachers shall by some magic of their own fit men to govern after the makers of laws and the preachers of civic ideals have had a free hand in writing the specifications. The reformers do not ask what men can be

[1] Logan Pearsall Smith.

taught. They say they should be taught whatever may be necessary to fit them to govern the modern world.

The usual appeal to education can bring only disappointment. For the problems of the modern world appear and change faster than any set of teachers can grasp them, much faster than they can convey their substance to a population of children. If the schools attempt to teach children how to solve the problems of the day, they are bound always to be in arrears. The most they can conceivably attempt is the teaching of a pattern of thought and feeling which will enable the citizen to approach a new problem in some useful fashion. But that pattern cannot be invented by the pedagogue. It is the political theorist's business to trace out that pattern. In that task he must not assume that the mass has political genius, but that men, even if they had genius, would give only a little time and attention to public affairs.

The moralist, I am afraid, will agree all too readily with the idea that social education must deal primarily not with the elements and solutions of particular phases of transient problems but with the principles that constitute an attitude toward all problems. I warn him off. It will require more than a good conscience to govern modern society, for conscience is no guide in situations where the essence of the difficulty is to find a guide for the conscience.

When I am tempted to think that men can be fitted out to deal with the modern world simply by teaching morals, manners and patriotism, I try to remember the fable of the pensive professor walking in the woods at twilight. He stumbled into a tree. This experience compelled him to act. Being a man of honor and breeding, he raised his hat, bowed deeply to the tree, and exclaimed with sincere regret: "Excuse me, sir, I thought you were a tree."

Is it fair, I ask, as a matter of morality, to

chide him for his conduct? If he had encountered a tree, can any one deny his right to
collide with it? If he had stumbled into a
man, was his apology not sufficient? Here
was a moral code in perfect working order,
and the only questionable aspect of his conduct
turned not on the goodness of his heart or
the firmness of his principles but on a point
of fact. You may retort that he had a moral
obligation to know the difference between a
man and a tree. Perhaps so. But suppose
that instead of walking in the woods he had
been casting a ballot; suppose that instead
of a tree he had encountered the Fordney-
McCumber tariff. How much more obligation
to know the truth would you have imposed
on him then? After all, this walker in the
woods at twilight with his mind on other
things was facing, as all of us think we are,
the facts he imagined were there, and was
doing his duty as he had learned it.

In some degree the whole animate world
seems to share the inexpertness of the thought-

ful professor. Pawlow showed by his experiments on dogs that an animal with a false stomach can experience all the pleasures of eating, and the number of mice and monkeys known to have been deceived in laboratories is surpassed only by the hopeful citizens of a democracy. Man's reflexes are, as the psychologists say, conditioned. And, therefore, he responds quite readily to a glass egg, a decoy duck, a stuffed shirt or a political platform. No moral code, as such, will enable him to know whether he is exercising his moral faculties on a real and an important event. For effective virtue, as Socrates pointed out long ago, is knowledge; and a code of the right and the wrong must wait upon a perception of the true and the false.

But even the successful practice of a moral code would not emancipate democracy. There are too many moral codes. In our immediate lives, within the boundaries of our own society, there may be commonly accepted standards. But a political theorist who asks that a local standard be universally applied is merely begging one of the questions he ought to be trying to solve. For, while possibly it may be an aim of political organization to arrive at a common standard of judgment, one of the conditions which engenders politics and makes political organization necessary is the conflict of standards.

Darwin's story of the cats and clover[2] may be recommended to any one who finds it difficult to free his mind of the assumption that his notions of good and bad are universal. The purple clover is cross-fertilized by the bumblebee, and, therefore, the more bumblebees the better next year's crop of clover. But the nests of bumblebees are rifled by field mice which are fond of the white grubs. Therefore, the more field mice the fewer bumblebees and the poorer the crop. But in the neighborhood of villages the cats hunt down the field mice. And so the more cats

[2] As told by J. Arthur Thomson, *The Outline of Science*, Vol. III, p. 646.

the fewer mice, the more bumblebees the better the crop. And the more kindly old ladies there are in the village the more cats there will be.

If you happen not to be a Hindu or a vegetarian and are a beef-eating Occidental you will commend the old ladies who keep the cats who hunt the mice who destroy the bumblebees who make the pasture of clover for the cattle. If you are a cat you also will be in favor of the old ladies. But if you are a field mouse, how different the rights and wrongs of that section of the universe! The old ladies who keep cats will seem about as kindly as witches with pet tigers, and the Old Lady Peril will be debated hysterically by the Field Mouse Security League. For what could a patriotic mouse think of a world in which bumblebees did not exist for the sole purpose of producing white grubs for field mice? There would seem to be no law and order in such a world; and only a highly philosophical mouse would admit with Bergson that "the idea of disorder objectifies for the convenience of language, the disappointment of a mind that finds before it an order different from what it wants." [3] For the order which we recognize as good is an order suited to our needs and hopes and habits.

There is nothing universal or eternal or unchangeable about our expectations. For rhetorical effect we often say there is. But in concrete cases it is not easy to explain why the thing we desire is so righteous. If the farmers are able to buy less than their accustomed amount of manufactured foods there is disorder and a problem. But what absolute standard is there which determines whether a bushel of wheat in 1925 should, as compared with 1913, exchange for more, as many, or less manufactures? Can any one define a principle which shall say whether the standard of living of the farmers or of any other class should rise or fall, and how fast and how much? There may be more jobs

[3] *Creative Evolution*, Ch. III.

than workingmen at the wage offered: the employers will complain and will call it a problem, but who knows any rule which tells how large a surplus of labor there ought to be and at what price? There may be more workingmen than jobs of the kind and at the places and for the wages they will or can take. But, although the problem will be acute, there is no principle which determines how many machinists, clerks, coal miners, bankers, or salesmen it is the duty of society to provide work for.

It requires intense partisanship and much self-deception to argue that some sort of peculiar righteousness adheres to the farmers' claims as against the manufacturers', the employers' against the wage-earners', the creditors' against the debtors', or the other way around. These conflicts of interest are problems. They require solution. But there is no moral pattern available from which the precise nature of the solution can be deduced.

If then eugenics cannot produce the ideal

democratic citizen, omnicompetent and sovereign, because biology knows neither how to breed political excellence nor what that excellence is; if education cannot equip the citizen, because the school teacher cannot anticipate the issues of the future; if morality cannot direct him, first, because right or wrong in specific cases depends upon the perception of true or false, and, second, on the assumption that there is a universal moral code, which, in fact, does not exist, where else shall we look for the method of making the competent citizen? Democratic theorists in the nineteenth century had several other prescriptions which still influence the thinking of many hopeful persons.

One school based their reforms on the aphorism that the cure for the evils of democracy is more democracy. It was assumed that the popular will was wise and good if only you could get at it. They proposed extensions of the suffrage, and as much voting as possible by means of the initiative, referendum and recall, direct election of Senators, direct primaries, an elected judiciary, and the like. They begged the question, for it has never been proved that there exists the kind of public opinion which they presupposed. Since the Bryan campaign of 1896 this school of thought has made great conquests in most of the states, and has profoundly influenced the federal government. The eligible vote has trebled since 1896; the direct action of the voter has been enormously extended. Yet that same period has seen a decline in the percentage of the popular vote cast at presidential elections from 80.75 per cent in 1896 to 52.36 per cent in 1920. Apparently there is a fallacy in the first assumption of this school that "the whole people" desires to participate actively in government. Nor is there any evidence to show that the persons who do participate are in any real sense directing the course of affairs. The party machines have survived every attack. And why should they not? If the voter cannot grasp the

details of the problems of the day because he
has not the time, the interest or the knowledge, he will not have a better public opinion
because he is asked to express his opinion
more often. He will simply be more bewildered, more bored and more ready to follow
along.

Another school, calling themselves revolutionary, have ascribed the disenchantment of
democracy to the capitalistic system. They
have argued that property is power, and that
until there is as wide a distribution of economic
power as there is of the right to vote the suffrage cannot be more effective. No serious
student, I think, would dispute that socialist
premise which asserts that the weight of influence on society exercised by an individual is
more nearly related to the character of his property than to his abstract legal citizenship. But
the socialist conclusion that economic power
can be distributed by concentrating the owner-
ship of great utilities in the state, the conclusion that the pervasion of industrial life

by voting and referenda will yield competent popular decisions, seems to me again to beg the question. For what reason is there to think that subjecting so many more affairs to the method of the vote will reveal hitherto undiscovered wisdom and technical competence and reservoirs of public interest in men? The socialist scheme has at its root the mystical fallacy of democracy, that the people, all of them, are competent; at its top it suffers from the homeopathic fallacy that adding new tasks to a burden the people will not and cannot carry now will make the burden of citizenship easily borne. The socialist theory presupposes an unceasing, untiring round of civic duties, an enormous complication of the political interests that are already much too complicated.

These various remedies, eugenic, educational, ethical, populist and socialist, all assume that either the voters are inherently competent to direct the course of affairs or that they are making progress toward such an ideal. I think it is a false ideal. I do not mean an undesirable ideal. I mean an unattainable ideal, bad only in the sense that it is bad for a fat man to try to be a ballet dancer. An ideal should express the true possibilities of its subject. When it does not it perverts the true possibilities. The ideal of the omnicompetent, sovereign citizen is, in my opinion, such a false ideal. It is unattainable. The pursuit of it is misleading. The failure to achieve it has produced the current disenchantment.

The individual man does not have opinions on all public affairs. He does not know how to direct public affairs. He does not know what is happening, why it is happening, what ought to happen. I cannot imagine how he could know, and there is not the least reason for thinking, as mystical democrats have thought, that the compounding of individual ignorances in masses of people can produce a continuous directing force in public affairs.

Chapter III

AGENTS AND BYSTANDERS

I

When a citizen has qualified as a voter he finds himself one of the theoretical rulers of a great going concern. He has not made the complicated machine with its five hundred thousand federal officers and its uncounted local offices. He has not seen much of it. He is bound by contracts, by debts, by treaties, by laws, made before he was aware of them. He does not from day to day decide who shall do what in the business of government. Only some small fraction of it comes intermittently to his notice. And in those episodic moments when he stands in the polling booth he is a highly intelligent and public-spirited voter indeed who can discover two real alternatives and enlist his influence

30

for a party which promises something he can understand.

The actual governing is made up of a multitude of arrangements on specific questions by particular individuals. These rarely become visible to the private citizen. Government, in the long intervals between elections, is carried on by politicians, officeholders and influential men who make settlements with other politicians, officeholders and influential men. The mass of people see these settlements, judge them, and affect them only now and then. They are altogether too numerous, too complicated, too obscure in their effects to become the subject of any continuing exercise of public opinion.

Nor in any exact and literal sense are those who conduct the daily business of government accountable after the fact to the great mass of the voters. They are accountable only, except in spectacular cases, to the other politicians, officeholders and influential men directly interested in the particular act.

Modern society is not visible to anybody, nor intelligible continuously and as a whole. One section is visible to another section, one series of acts is intelligible to this group and another to that.

Even this degree of responsible understanding is attainable only by the development of fact-finding agencies of great scope and complexity.[1] These agencies give only a remote and incidental assistance to the general public. Their findings are too intricate for the casual reader. They are also almost always much too uninteresting. Indeed the popular boredom and contempt for the expert and for statistical measurement are such that the organization of intelligence to administer modern affairs would probably be entirely neglected were it not that departments of government, corporations, trade unions and trade associations are being compelled by their own internal necessities of administration, and by compulsion of other corporate groups, to

[1] *Cf.* my *Public Opinion*, Chapters XXV and XXVI.

record their own acts, measure them, publish them and stand accountable for them.

The need in the Great Society not only for publicity but for uninterrupted publicity is indisputable. But we shall misunderstand the need seriously if we imagine that the purpose of the publication can possibly be the informing of every voter. We live at the mere beginnings of public accounting. Yet the facts far exceed our curiosity. The railroads, for example, make an accounting. Do we read the results? Hardly. A few executives here and there, some bankers, some regulating officials, some representatives of shippers and the like read them. The rest of us ignore them for the good and sufficient reason that we have other things to do.

For the man does not live who can read all the reports that drift across his doorstep or all the dispatches in his newspaper. And if by some development of the radio every man could see and hear all that was happening everywhere, if publicity, in other words, became absolute, how much time could or would he spend watching the Sinking Fund Commission and the Geological Survey? He would probably tune in on the Prince of Wales, or, in desperation, throw off the switch and seek peace in ignorance. It is bad enough today— with morning newspapers published in the evening and evening newspapers in the morning, with October magazines in September, with the movies and the radio—to be condemned to live under a barrage of eclectic information, to have one's mind made the receptacle for a hullabaloo of speeches, arguments and unrelated episodes. General information for the informing of public opinion is altogether too general for intellectual decency. And life is too short for the pursuit of omniscience by the counting in a state of nervous excitement of all the leaves on all the trees.

2

If all men had to conceive the whole process of government all the time the world's work would obviously never be carried on. Men make no attempt to consider society as a whole. The farmer decides whether to plant wheat or corn, the mechanic whether to take the job offered at the Pennsylvania or the Erie shops, whether to buy a Ford or a piano, and, if a Ford, whether to buy it from the garage on Elm Street or from the dealer who sent him a circular. These decisions are among fairly narrow choices offered to him; he can no more choose among all the jobs in the world than he can consider marrying any woman in the world. These choices in detail are in their cumulative mass the government of society. They may rest on ignorant or enlightened opinions, but, whether he comes to them by accident or scientific instruction, they are specific and particular among at best a few concrete alternatives and they lead to a definite, visible result.

But men are supposed also to hold public opinions about the general conduct of society. The mechanic is supposed not only to choose

between working for the Pennsylvania or the
Erie but to decide how in the interests of
the nation all the railroads of the country
shall be regulated. The two kinds of opinion
merge insensibly one into the other; men have
general notions which influence their individual decisions and their direct experiences unconsciously govern their general notions. Yet
it is useful to distinguish between the two
kinds of opinion, the specific and direct, the
general and the indirect.

Specific opinions give rise to immediate
executive acts; to take a job, to do a particular
piece of work, to hire or fire, to buy or sell, to
stay here or go there, to accept or refuse, to
command or obey. General opinions give
rise to delegated, indirect, symbolic, intangible
results: to a vote, to a resolution, to ap-
plause, to criticism, to praise or dispraise,
to audiences, circulations, followings, con-
tentment or discontent. The specific opinion
may lead to a decision to act within the
area where a man has personal jurisdiction;

that is, within the limits set by law and custom, his personal power and his personal desire. But general opinions lead only to some sort of expression, such as voting, and do not result in executive acts except in coöperation with the general opinions of large numbers of other persons.

Since the general opinions of large numbers of persons are almost certain to be a vague and confusing medley, action cannot be taken until these opinions have been factored down, canalized, compressed and made uniform. The making of one general will out of a multitude of general wishes is not an Hegelian mystery, as so many social philosophers have imagined, but an art well known to leaders, politicians and steering committees.[2] It consists essentially in the use of symbols which assemble emotions after they have been detached from their ideas. Because feelings are much less specific than ideas, and yet more poignant, the leader is able to make a

[2] *Cf.* my *Public Opinion*, Chapters XIII and XIV.

homogeneous will out of a heterogeneous mass of desires. The process, therefore, by which general opinions are brought to co-operation consists of an intensification of feeling and a degradation of significance. Before a mass of general opinions can eventuate in executive action, the choice is narrowed down to a few alternatives. The victorious alternative is executed not by the mass but by individuals in control of its energy.

A private opinion may be quite complicated, and may issue in quite complicated actions, in a whole train of subsidiary opinions, as when a man decides to build a house and then makes a hundred judgments as to how it shall be built. But a public opinion has no such immediate responsibility or continuous result. It leads in politics to the making of a pencil mark on a piece of paper, and then to a period of waiting and watching as to whether one or two years hence the mark shall be made in the same column or in the adjoining one. The decision to make the mark may be for reasons a^1, a^2, a^3 . . . a^n: the result, whether an idiot or genius has voted, is A.

For great masses of people, though each of them may have more or less distinct views, must when they act converge to an identical result. And the more complex the collection of men the more ambiguous must be the unity and the simpler the common ideas.

3

In English-speaking countries during the last century the contrast between the action of men individually and in the mass has been much emphasized, and yet greatly misunderstood. Macaulay, for example, speaking on the Reform Bill of 1832, drew the conventional distinction between private enterprise and public action:

"In all those things which depend on the intelligence, the knowledge, the industry, the energy of individuals, this country stands preëminent among all countries of the world

ancient and modern. But in those things
which it belongs to the state to direct we have
no such claim to superiority . . . can there be
a stronger contrast than that which exists
between the beauty, the completeness, the
speed, the precision with which every process
is performed in our factories, and the awkward-
ness, the crudeness, the slowness, the uncer-
tainty of the apparatus by which offenses
are punished and rights vindicated? . . .
Surely we see the barbarism of the Thirteenth
Century and the highest civilization of the
Nineteenth Century side by side, and we see
that the barbarism belongs to the government,
and the civilization to the people."[3]

Macaulay was, of course, thinking of the
contrast between factory production and
government as it existed in England under
Queen Victoria's uncles and the hard-drink-
ing, hard-riding squirearchy. But the Prus-
sian bureaucracy amply demonstrated that

[3] Speech on the Reform Bill of 1832, quoted in the *Times* (London),
July 12, 1923.

there is no such necessary contrast between governmental and private action. There is a contrast between action by and through great masses of people and action that moves without them.

The fundamental contrast is not between public and private enterprises, between "crowd" psychology and individual, but between men doing specific things and men attempting to command general results. The work of the world is carried on by men in their executive capacity, by an infinite number of concrete acts, plowing and planting and reaping, building and destroying, fitting this to that, going from here to there, transforming A into B and moving B from X to Y. The relationships between the individuals doing these specific things are balanced by a most intricate mechanism of exchange, of contract, of custom and of implied promises. Where men are performing their work they must learn to understand the process and the substance of these obligations if they are to do it at all. But in governing the work of other men by votes or by the expression of opinion they can only reward or punish a result, accept or reject alternatives presented to them. They can say yes or no to something which has been done, yes or no to a proposal, but they cannot create, administer and actually perform the act they have in mind. Persons uttering public opinions may now and then be able to define the acts of men, but their opinions do not execute these acts.

4

To the realm of executive acts, each of us, as a member of the public, remains always external. Our public opinions are always and forever, by their very nature, an attempt to control the actions of others from the outside. If we can grasp the full significance of that conclusion we shall, I think, have found a way of fixing the rôle of public opinion in its true perspective; we shall know how to account for the disenchantment of democ-

racy, and we shall begin to see the outline of
an ideal of public opinion which, unlike that
accepted in the dogma of democracy, may be
really attainable.

CHAPTER IV

WHAT THE PUBLIC DOES

I

I DO not mean to say that there is no other attainable ideal of public opinion but that severely practical one which this essay is meant to disclose. One might aim to enrich the minds of men with charming fantasies, animate nature and society with spirits, set up an Olympus in the skies and an Atlantis at the end of the world. And one might then assert that, so the quality of ideas be fine or give peace, it does not matter how or whether they eventuate in the government of affairs.

Utopia and Nirvana are by definition their own sufficient reason, and it may be that to contemplate them is well worth the abandonment of feeble attempts to control the action of events. Renunciation, however, is a luxury in which all men cannot indulge. They will

44

somehow seek to control the behavior of others, if not by positive law then at least by persuasion. When men are in that posture toward events they are a public, as I am here defining the term; their opinions as to how others ought to behave are public opinions. The more clearly it is understood what the public can do and what it cannot, the more effectively it will do what lies within its power to do well and the less it will interfere with the liberties of men.

The rôle of public opinion is determined by the fact that its relation to a problem is external. The opinion affects an opinion, but does not itself control the executive act. A public opinion is expressed by a vote, a demonstration of praise or blame, a following or a boycotting. But these manifestations are in themselves nothing. They count only if they influence the course of affairs. They influence it, however, only if they influence an actor in the affair. And it is, I believe, precisely in this secondary, indirect relationship between public opinion and public affairs that we have the clue to the limits and the possibilities of public opinion.

2

It may be objected at once that an election which turns one set of men out of office and installs another is an expression of public opinion which is neither secondary nor indirect. But what in fact is an election? We call it an expression of the popular will. But is it? We go into a polling booth and mark a cross on a piece of paper for one of two, or perhaps three or four names. Have we expressed our thoughts on the public policy of the United States? Presumably we have a number of thoughts on this and that with many buts and ifs and ors. Surely the cross on a piece of paper does not express them. It would take us hours to express our thoughts, and calling a vote the expression of our mind is an empty fiction.

A vote is a promise of support. It is a

way of saying: I am lined up with these men, on this side. I enlist with them. I will follow. I will buy. I will boycott. I will strike. I applaud. I jeer. The force I can exert is placed here, not there.

The public does not select the candidate, write the platform, outline the policy any more than it builds the automobile or acts the play. It aligns itself for or against somebody who has offered himself, has made a promise, has produced a play, is selling an automobile. The action of a group as a group is the mobilization of the force it possesses.

The attempt has been made to ascribe some intrinsic moral and intellectual virtue to majority rule. It was said often in the nineteenth century that there was a deep wisdom in majorities which was the voice of God. Sometimes this flattery was a sincere mysticism, sometimes it was the self-deception which always accompanies the idealization of power. In substance it was nothing but a transfer to the new sovereign of the divine attributes of kings. Yet the inherent absurdity of making virtue and wisdom dependent on 51 per cent of any collection of men has always been apparent. The practical realization that the claim was absurd has resulted in a whole code of civil rights to protect minorities and in all sorts of elaborate methods of subsidizing the arts and sciences and other human interests so they might be independent of the operation of majority rule.

The justification of majority rule in politics is not to be found in its ethical superiority. It is to be found in the sheer necessity of finding a place in civilized society for the force which resides in the weight of numbers. I have called voting an act of enlistment, an alignment for or against, a mobilization. These are military metaphors, and rightly so, I think, for an election based on the principle of majority rule is historically and practically a sublimated and denatured civil war, a paper mobilization without physical violence.

Constitutional democrats, in the intervals when they were not idealizing the majority, have acknowledged that a ballot was a civilized substitute for a bullet. "The French Revolution," says Bernard Shaw, "overthrew one set of rulers and substituted another with different interests and different views. That is what a general election enables the people to do in England every seven years if they choose. Revolution is therefore a national institution in England; and its advocacy by an Englishman needs no apology." [1] It makes an enormous difference, of course, whether the people fight or vote, but we shall understand the nature of voting better if we recognize it to be a substitute for fighting. "There grew up in the 17th and 18th Centuries in England," says Dwight Morrow in his introduction to Professor Morse's book, "and there has been carried from England to almost every civilized government in the world, a procedure through which party

[1] Preface to *The Revolutionist's Handbook*, p. 179.

government becomes in large measure a substitute for revolution." [2] Hans Delbrück puts the matter simply when he says that the principle of majority rule is "a purely practical principle. If one wants to avoid a civil war, one lets those rule who in any case would obtain the upper hand if there should be a struggle; and they are the superior numbers." [3]

But, while an election is in essence sublimated warfare, we must take care not to miss the importance of the sublimation. There have been pedantic theorists who wished to disqualify all who could not bear arms, and woman suffrage has been deplored as a falsification of the value of an election in uncovering the alignment of martial force in the community. One can safely ignore such theorizing. For, while the institution of an election is in its historical origins an alignment of the physical force, it has come to be an align-

---

[2] *Parties and Party Leaders*, p. xvi.

[3] H. Delbrück, *Government and the Will of the People*, p. 15. Translated by Roy S. MacElwee.

ment of all kinds of force. It remains an alignment, though in advanced democracies it has lost most of its primitive association with military combat. It has not lost it in the South where the Negro population is disfranchised by force, and not permitted to make its weight felt in an election. It has not lost it in the unstable Latin American republics where every election is in some measure still an armed revolution. In fact, the United States has officially recognized this truth by proclaiming that the substitution of election for revolution in Central America is the test of political progress.

I do not wish to labor the argument any further than may be necessary to establish the theory that what the public does is not to express its opinions but to align itself for or against a proposal. If that theory is accepted, we must abandon the notion that democratic government can be the direct expression of the will of the people. We must abandon the notion that the people govern.

Instead we must adopt the theory that, by their occasional mobilizations as a majority, people support or oppose the individuals who actually govern. We must say that the popular will does not direct continuously but that it intervenes occasionally.

Chapter V

THE NEUTRALIZATION OF ARBITRARY FORCE

I

IF THIS is the nature of public action, what ideal can be formulated which shall conform to it?

We are bound, I think, to express the ideal in its lowest terms, to state it not as an ideal which might conceivably be realized by exceptional groups now and then or in some distant future but as an ideal which normally might be taught and attained. In estimating the burden which a public can carry, a sound political theory must insist upon the largest factor of safety. It must understate the possibilities of public action.

The action of a public, we had concluded, is principally confined to an occasional intervention in affairs by means of an alignment of the force which a dominant section of that public can wield. We must assume, then, that the members of a public will not possess an insider's knowledge of events or share his point of view. They cannot, therefore, construe intent, or appraise the exact circumstances, enter intimately into the minds of the actors or into the details of the argument. They can watch only for coarse signs indicating where their sympathies ought to turn.

We must assume that the members of a public will not anticipate a problem much before its crisis has become obvious, nor stay with the problem long after its crisis is past. They will not know the antecedent events, will not have seen the issue as it developed, will not have thought out or willed a program, and will not be able to predict the consequences of acting on that program. We must assume as a theoretically fixed premise of popular government that normally men as members of a public will not be well informed, continuously interested, nonpartisan, creative or executive. We must assume that a public is inexpert in its curiosity, intermittent, that it discerns only gross distinctions, is slow to be aroused and quickly diverted; that, since it acts by aligning itself, it personalizes whatever it considers, and is interested only when events have been melodramatized as a conflict.

The public will arrive in the middle of the third act and will leave before the last curtain, having stayed just long enough perhaps to decide who is the hero and who the villain of the piece. Yet usually that judgment will necessarily be made apart from the intrinsic merits, on the basis of a sample of behavior, an aspect of a situation, by very rough external evidence.

We cannot, then, think of public opinion as a conserving or creating force directing society to clearly conceived ends, making deliberately toward socialism or away from it, toward nationalism, an empire, a league of nations or any other doctrinal goal.   For

men do not agree as to their aims, and it is
precisely the lack of agreement which creates
the problems that excite public attention.
It is idle, then, to argue that though men evi-
dently have conflicting purposes, mankind
has some all-embracing purpose of which you
or I happen to be the authorized spokesman.
We merely should have moved in a circle were
we to conclude that the public is in some deep
way a messianic force.

2

The work of the world goes on continually
without conscious direction from public opinion.   At certain junctures problems arise.
It is only with the crises of some of these
problems that public opinion is concerned.
And its object in dealing with a crisis is to
help allay that crisis.

I think this conclusion is unescapable. For
though we may prefer to believe that the
aim of popular action should be to do justice
or promote the true, the beautiful and the

good, the belief will not maintain itself in the face of plain experience. The public does not know in most crises what specifically is the truth or the justice of the case, and men are not agreed on what is beautiful and good. Nor does the public rouse itself normally at the existence of evil. It is aroused at evil made manifest by the interruption of a habitual process of life. And finally, a problem ceases to occupy attention not when justice, as we happen to define it, has been done but when a workable adjustment that overcomes the crisis has been made. If all this were not the necessary manner of public opinion, if it had seriously to crusade for justice in every issue it touches, the public would have to be dealing with all situations all the time. That is impossible. It is also undesirable. For did justice, truth, goodness and beauty depend on the spasmodic and crude interventions of public opinion there would be little hope for them in this world.

Thus we strip public opinion of any implied

duty to deal with the substance of a problem, to make technical decisions, to attempt justice or impose a moral precept. And instead we say that the ideal of public opinion is to align men during the crisis of a problem in such a way as to favor the action of those individuals who may be able to compose the crisis. The power to discern those individuals is the end of the effort to educate public opinion. The aim of research designed to facilitate public action is the discovery of clear signs by which these individuals may be discerned.

The signs are relevant when they reveal by coarse, simple and objective tests which side in a controversy upholds a workable social rule, or which is attacking an unworkable rule, or which proposes a promising new rule. By following such signs the public might know where to align itself. In such an alignment it does not, let us remember, pass judgment on the intrinsic merits. It merely places its force at the disposal of the side which, according to objective signs, seems to be standing for human adjustments according to a clear rule of behavior and against the side which appears to stand for settlement in accordance with its own unaccountable will.

Public opinion, in this theory, is a reserve of force brought into action during a crisis in public affairs. Though it is itself an irrational force, under favorable institutions, sound leadership and decent training the power of public opinion might be placed at the disposal of those who stood for workable law as against brute assertion. In this theory, public opinion does not make the law. But by canceling lawless power it may establish the condition under which law can be made. It does not reason, investigate, invent, persuade, bargain or settle. But, by holding the aggressive party in check, it may liberate intelligence. Public opinion in its highest ideal will defend those who are prepared to act on their reason against the interrupting force of those who merely assert their will.

The action of public opinion at its best

would not, let it be noted, be a continual crusade on behalf of reason. When power, however absolute and unaccountable, reigns without provoking a crisis, public opinion does not challenge it. Somebody must challenge arbitrary power first. The public can only come to his assistance.

3

That, I think, is the utmost that public opinion can effectively do. With the substance of the problem it can do nothing usually but meddle ignorantly or tyrannically. It has no need to meddle with it. Men in their active relation to affairs have to deal with the substance, but in that indirect relationship when they can act only through uttering praise or blame, making black crosses on white paper, they have done enough, they have done all they can do if they help to make it possible for the reason of other men to assert itself.

For when public opinion attempts to govern

directly it is either a failure or a tyranny. It is not able to master the problem intellectually, nor to deal with it except by wholesale impact. The theory of democracy has not recognized this truth because it has identified the functioning of government with the will of the people. This is a fiction. The intricate business of framing laws and of administering them through several hundred thousand public officials is in no sense the act of the voters nor a translation of their will.

But although the acts of government are not a translation of public opinion, the principal function of government is to do specifically, in greater detail, and more continually what public opinion does crudely, by wholesale, and spasmodically. It enforces some of the working rules of society. It interprets them. It detects and punishes certain kinds of aggression. It presides over the framing of new rules. It has organized force which is used to counteract irregular force.

It is also subject to the same corruption as

public opinion. For when government attempts to impose the will of its officials, instead of intervening so as to steady adjustments by consent among the parties directly interested, it becomes heavy-handed, stupid, imperious, even predatory. For the public official, though he is better placed to understand the problem than a reader of newspapers, and though he is much better able to act, is still fundamentally external to the real problems in which he intervenes. Being external, his point of view is indirect, and so his action is most appropriate when it is confined to rendering indirect assistance to those who are directly responsible.

Therefore, instead of describing government as an expression of the people's will, it would seem better to say that government consists of a body of officials, some elected, some appointed, who handle professionally, and in the first instance, problems which come to public opinion spasmodically and on appeal. Where the parties directly responsible do not work out an adjustment, public officials intervene. When the officials fail, public opinion is brought to bear on the issue.

4

This, then, is the ideal of public action which our inquiry suggests. Those who happen in any question to constitute the public should attempt only to create an equilibrium in which settlements can be reached directly and by consent. The burden of carrying on the work of the world, of inventing, creating, executing, of attempting justice, formulating laws and moral codes, of dealing with the technic and the substance, lies not upon public opinion and not upon government but on those who are responsibly concerned as agents in the affair. Where problems arise, the ideal is a settlement by the particular interests involved. They alone know what the trouble really is. No decision by public officials or by commuters reading headlines in the train can usually and in the long run be so good as settlement by consent among the parties at interest. No moral code, no political theory can usually and in the long run be imposed from the heights of public opinion, which will fit a case so well as direct agreement reached where arbitrary power has been disarmed.

It is the function of public opinion to check the use of force in a crisis, so that men, driven to make terms, may live and let live.

PART II

Chapter VI

THE QUESTION ARISTOTLE ASKED

THESE conclusions are sharply at variance with the accepted theory of popular government. That theory rests upon the belief that there is a public which directs the course of events. I hold that this public is a mere phantom. It is an abstraction. The public in respect to a railroad strike may be the farmers whom the railroad serves; the public in respect to an agricultural tariff may include the very railroad men who were on strike. The public is not, as I see it, a fixed body of individuals. It is merely those persons who are interested in an affair and can affect it only by supporting or opposing the actors.

Since these random publics cannot be expected to deal with the merits of a controversy, they can give their support with reasonable assurance that it will do good only if there are easily recognizable and yet pertinent signs which they can follow. Are there such signs? Can they be discovered? Can they be formulated so they might be learned and used? The chapters of this second part are an attempt to answer these questions.

The signs must be of such a character that they can be recognized without any substantial insight into the substance of a problem. Yet they must be relevant to the solution of the problem. They must be signs which will tell the members of a public where they can best align themselves so as to promote the solution. In short, they must be guides to reasonable action for the use of uninformed people.

The environment is complex. Man's political capacity is simple. Can a bridge be built between them? The question has haunted political science ever since Aristotle first formulated it in the great seventh book of his *Politics*. He answered it by saying that the community must be kept simple and small enough to suit the faculties of its citizens.

We who live in the Great Society are unable to follow his advice. The orthodox democrats answered Aristotle's question by assuming that a limitless political capacity resides in public opinion. A century of experience compels us to deny this assumption. For us, then, the old question is unanswered; we can neither reject the Great Society as Aristotle did, nor exaggerate the political capacity of the citizen as the democrats did. We are forced to ask whether it is possible for men to find a way of acting effectively upon highly complex affairs by very simple means.

I venture to think that this problem may be soluble, that principles can be elucidated which might effect a successful junction between the intricacies of the environment and the simplicities of human faculty. It goes without saying that what I shall present here is no final statement of these principles. At most and at best it may be a clue, with some illustrations, that can be developed by research. But even that much assurance seems to me rash in the light of the difficulties which the problem has always presented, and so, following Descartes, I add that "after all, it is possible I may be mistaken; and it is but a little copper and glass I take for gold and diamonds." [1]

[1] *Discourse on Method*, Part I.

Chapter VII

THE NATURE OF A PROBLEM

I

SOMEWHAT in the spirit of Descartes, let us begin by supposing that your whole experience were confined to one glimpse of the world. There would be, I think, no better or worse in your sight, neither good men nor bad, patriots nor profiteers, conservatives nor radicals. You would be a perfect neutral. From such an impression of things, it would never occur to you that the crest of a mountain endured longer than the crest of a wave, that people moved about and that trees did not, or that the roar of an orator would pass sooner than the roar of Niagara.

Lengthen your experience, and you would begin to notice differences in the constancy of things. You would know day and night, perhaps, but not winter and summer, movement in space, but little of age in time. And if you then formulated your social philosophy, would you not almost certainly conclude that the things you saw people doing then it was ordained they should do always, and that their characters as you had seen them that day would be thus and so forever? And would not the resulting treatise pass almost unnoticed in any collection of contemporary disquisitions on the nations, the races, the classes or the sexes?

But the more you lengthened the span of your impression, the more variability you would note, until at last you would say with Heraclitus that all things flow. For when the very stars and the rocks were seen to have a history, men and their institutions and customs, habits and ideals, theories and policies could seem only relatively permanent. And you would have to conclude that what at first glance you had called a constant turns out after you had watched it longer merely

to be changing a little more slowly than
something else.

With sufficiently long experience you would
indeed be bound to conclude that while the
diverse elements that bear upon the life of
men, including the characters of men themselves, were changing, yet they were not
changing at the same pace. Things multiply,
they grow, they learn, they age, they wear out
and they die at different rates. An individual,
his companions, his implements, his institutions, his creeds, his needs, his means of satisfaction, evolve unevenly, and endure unevenly. Events do not concur harmoniously
in time. Some hurry, some straggle, some
push and some drag. The ranks have always
to be reformed.

Instead of that one grand system of evolution and progress, which the nineteenth century found so reassuring, there would appear
to be innumerable systems of evolution,
variously affecting each other, some linked,
some in collision, but each in some funda-

mental aspect moving at its own pace and on its own terms.

The disharmonies of this uneven evolution are the problems of mankind.

2

Suppose a man who knew nothing of the history of the nineteenth century were shown the tables compiled in the *Statistical Abstract of the United States* for the period from 1800 to 1918: He would note that the population of the world had multiplied two and a half times; its total commerce 42 times; its shipping tonnage more than 7 times; its railways 3664 times; its telegraphs 317 times; its cotton production 17 times; its coal 113 times; its pig iron 77 times. Could he doubt that in a century of such uneven changes men had faced revolutionary social problems?

Could he not infer from these figures alone that there had been great movements of population, vast changes in men's occupation, in the character of their labor, their wants, their standards of living, their ambitions? Would he not fairly infer that the political system which had existed in 1800 must have altered vastly with these new relationships, that customs, manners and morals appropriate to the settled, small and more or less self-contained communities of 1800 had been subjected to new strains and had probably been thoroughly revised? As he imagined the realities behind the tables, would he not infer that as men lived through the changes which these cold figures summarize they had been in conflict with their old habits and ideals, that the process of making new habits and adjustments must have gone on subject to trial and error with hopefulness over material progress and yet much disorder and confusion of soul?

3

For a more specific illustration of the nature of a problem we may examine the problem of population in its simplest form. When Malthus first stated it he assumed, for the purposes of argument, two elements evolving at different rates. Population, he said, doubled every twenty-five years; the produce of land could be increased in the same time by an amount "equal to what it at present produces."[1] He was writing about the year 1800. The population of England he estimated at seven millions, and the food supply as adequate to that number. There was then, in 1800, no problem. By 1825 the population, according to his estimate of its rate of increase, would have doubled, but the food supply would also have doubled. There would be no problem of population. But by 1850 the population would stand at twenty-eight millions; the food supply would have increased only by an amount to support an additional seven millions. The problem of excess population, or, if you like, of food scarcity, would have appeared. For while in 1800 and in 1825 the food available for each person would be the same, in 1850,

[1] T. R. Malthus, *An Essay on the Principle of Population*, Chapter II.

owing to the uneven rate of growth, there would be only a three-quarter ration for each person. And this altered relationship Malthus rightly called a problem.

Suppose, now, we complicate Malthus's argument a bit by assuming that in 1850 people had learned to eat less and felt more fit on the three-quarter ration. There would then be no problem in 1850, for the adjustment of the two variables—food and people— would be satisfactory. Or, on the contrary, suppose that soon after 1800 people had demanded a higher standard of living and expected more food, though the necessary additional food was not produced. These new demands would create a problem. Or suppose, as was actually the case,[2] the food supply increased faster than Malthus had assumed it could, though population did not. The problem of population would not arise at the date he predicted. Or suppose the increase of population was reduced by birth

[2] A. M. Carr-Saunders, *The Population Problem*, p. 28.

control. The problem, as Malthus first stated it, would not arise.[3] Or suppose the food supply increased faster than the population could consume it. There would then be a problem not of population but of agricultural surplus.

In an absolutely static society there would be no problems. A problem is the result of change. But not of the change in any self-contained element. Change would be unnoticeable unless we could measure it against some other element which did not change at the same pace. If everything in the universe expanded at a mile a minute, or shrank at the same rate, we should never know it. For all we can tell we may be the size of a mosquito one moment in the sight of God, and of an elephant the next; we cannot tell if mosquitoes and elephants and chairs and planets change in proportion. Change is significant only in relation to something else.

The change which constitutes a problem

[3] Malthus himself recognized this in a later edition of his book.

is an altered relationship between two dependent variables.[4] Thus the automobile is a problem in the city not because there are so many automobiles but because there are too many for the width of the streets, too many for the number of competent drivers, because the too narrow streets are filled with too many cars driven too recklessly for the present ability of the police to control them. Because the automobile is manufactured faster than old city streets can be widened, because some persons acquire cars faster than they acquire prudence and good manners, because automobiles collect in cities faster than policemen can be recruited, trained or paid for by slow-yielding taxpayers, there is an automobile problem made evident by crowding, obnoxious fumes and collisions.

But though these evils seem to arise from the automobile, the fault lies not in the automobile but in the relation between the auto-

[4] *Cf.* in this connection W. F. Ogburn, *Social Change, passim,* but particularly Part IV, 1, on "The Hypothesis of Cultural Lag."

mobile and the city. This may sound like splitting hairs, but unless we insist upon it we never define a problem accurately nor lay it open successfully to solution.

The problem of national defense, for example, can never be stated by a general staff which draws upon its inner consciousness for an estimate of the necessary force. The necessary force can be estimated only in relation to the probable enemy, and the military problem whether of peace or of war lies always in the ratio of forces. Military force is a purely relative conception. The British Navy is helpless as a child against the unarmed mountaineers of Tibet. The French Army has no force as against fishing smacks in the Pacific Ocean. Force has to be measured against its objective: the tiger and the shark are incomparable one with the other.

Now a settled and accepted ratio of forces that might collide is a state of military peace. A competitive and, therefore, constantly unbalanced ratio is a prelude to war. The Canadian border presents no military problem, not because Canada's forces and our own are equal but because, happily, we do not compare them. They are independent variables, having no relation one with the other, and a change in the one does not affect the other. In capital ships we are confronted now with no naval problem in the Atlantic or in the Pacific, because with Britain and Japan, the only two comparable powers, we are agreed on a ratio by treaty.[5] But for all types of ships not subject to the ratio there is a naval problem in both oceans, and if the Washington Treaty should lapse the problem which it settled would recur. It would recur because the synchronized progress of the three navies would be replaced by a relatively uneven progress of each as compared with the others.

[5] However, the controversy over gun elevation demonstrates how difficult it is to maintain an equilibrium of force where so many factors are variable.

4

The field of economic activity is the source
of many problems. For, as Cassel says,[6] we
include within the meaning of the word economic those means of satisfying human wants
which are "usually available only in a limited
quantity." Since "the wants of civilized
human beings as a whole are," for all practical
purposes, "unlimited," there is in all economic
life the constant necessity of reaching "an
adjustment between the wants and the means
of supplying the wants." This disharmony
of supply and demand is the source of an
unending series of problems.

We may note at once that the economist
does not claim as his province the whole
range of adjustments between human wants
and the means of satisfying them. He usually
omits, for example, the human need to
breathe air. For since the air is unlimited in
quantity the human need of it is not frus-

[6] Gustav Cassel, *A Theory of Social Economy*, Chapter I.

trated, and the surplus air not required by men in no way impinges upon their lives. Yet there may be a scarcity of air, as, for example, in a congested tenement district. Then an economic problem is engendered which has to be met, let us say, by building laws requiring a certain number of cubic feet of air a person. The economist, in other words, takes as his field of interest the maladjustment between human wants and those means of satisfying them which are available, but only in limited quantities. In a world where every want was satisfied there would be no problems for him; nor any in a world where men had no wants; nor any in a world where the only wants men had could be supplied by a change on their part of their own states of consciousness. To create a problem there must be at least two dependent but separated variables: wants and the means of satisfaction; and these two variables must have a disposition to alter so that an antecedent equilibrium is disturbed.

In the measure, says Cassel, in which the

economic system succeeds in securing an adjustment between the wants and the means of supplying the wants we speak of it as a sound economy. "This task may be accomplished in three different ways: first, by eliminating the less important wants and so restricting the total wants; secondly, by making the best possible use of the means available for the purposes in question; and, thirdly, by increased personal exertions."[7]

Since the problem arises out of the disharmony of supply and demand, its solution is to be found by increasing the supply or restricting the demand. The choice of method depends first of all on which it is possible in specific cases to follow, and, second, granting the possibility, on which is the easier or the preferred. Either method will give what we acknowledge as a solution. For when two variables are in an adjustment which does not frustrate the expectations of either there is no problem, and none will be felt to exist.

[7] *Ibid.*, p. 7.

CHAPTER VIII

SOCIAL CONTRACTS

I

IT IS impossible to imagine in the universe a harmony of all things, each with all the others. The only harmonies we know or can conceive, outside of what Mr. Santayana calls the realm of essences, are partial adjustments which sacrifice to some one end all purposes which conflict with it. That the tree may bear fruit for us, we readily kill the insects that eat the fruit. So the fruit will ripen for us, we take no account of the disharmony we create for innumerable flies.

In the light of eternity it may be wholly unimportant whether the harmonies on this earth are suited to men or to insects. For in the light of eternity and from the point of view of the universe as a whole nothing can be what we call good or bad, better or worse.

All ideas of value are measurements of some part of this universe with some other part, and it is no more possible to value the universe as a whole than it is to weigh it as a whole. For all scales of value and of weight are contained within it. To judge the whole universe you must, like a god, be outside of it, a point of view no mortal mind can adopt.

Unfortunately for the fly, therefore, we are bound to judge him by human values. In so far as we have power over him, he must submit to the harmonies we seek to establish. We may as a sporting matter admit his theoretical right to establish his own harmonies against us if he can, and to call them better if he likes, but for us that only is good which is good for man. Our universe consists of all that it contains, not as such, not as the fly knows it, but in its relation to us. From any other point of view but man's, his conception of the universe is askew. It has an emphasis and a perspective, it is shaped to a design which is altogether human. The very forms, colors, odors and sound of things are dependent for their quality upon our sense organs. Their relations are seen and understood against the background of our necessities.

In the realm of man's interests and purposes and desires, the perspectives are even narrower. There is no human point of view here, but only the points of view of men. None is valid for all human beings, none for all of human history, none for all corners of the globe. An opinion of the right and the wrong, the good and the bad, the pleasant and the unpleasant, is dated, is localized, is relative. It applies only to some men at some time in some place under some circumstances.

2

Against this deep pluralism thinkers have argued in vain. They have invented social organisms and national souls, and oversouls, and collective souls; they have gone for hopeful analogies to the beehive and the anthill, to the solar system, to the human body; they

have gone to Hegel for higher unities and to
Rousseau for a general will in an effort to
find some basis of union. For though men
do not think alike, nor want the same things,
though their private interests are so distinct
that they do not merge easily in any common
interest, yet men cannot live by themselves,
nor realize even their private purposes without
taking into account the behavior of other
people. We, however, no longer expect to find
a unity which absorbs diversity. For us the
conflicts and differences are so real that we
cannot deny them and instead of looking for
identity of purpose we look simply for an
accommodation of purposes.

When we speak, then, about the solution of
a problem in the Great Society, we may mean
little more than that two conflicting interests
have found a *modus vivendi*. It may be, of
course, that they have really removed all their
differences, that one interest has yielded to
the other, or both to a third. But the solutions of most social problems are not so neat

as this; everything does not fit perfectly as in the solution of a puzzle. The conflicting interests merely find a way of giving a little and taking a little, and of existing together without too much bad blood.

They still remain separate interests. The men involved still think differently. They have no union of mind or purpose. But they travel their own ways without collision, and even with some reliance at times upon the others' help. They know their rights and their duties, what to expect and what will be expected. Their rights are usually less than they claim, and their duties heavier than they like, yet, because they are in some degree enforced, conduct is rendered intelligible and predictable, and coöperation exists in spite of the conflicting interests of men.

The *modus vivendi* of any particular historical period, the system of rights and duties, has generally acquired some high religious or ideal sanction. The thinkers laureate of the age will generally manage to show that the

institutions, the laws, the morality and the
custom of that age are divinely inspired.
These are tiresome illusions which have
been exploded a thousand times. The prevailing system of rights and duties at any
time is at bottom a slightly antiquated formulation of the balance of power among the
active interests in the community. There is
always a certain lag, as Mr. Ogburn calls it,
so that the system of rights and duties men
are taught is generally a little less contemporary than the system they would find most
convenient. But, whether the system is ob-
solete or not, in its naked origin, a right is
a claim somebody was able to assert, and a
duty is an obligation somebody was able to
impose.

3

The prevailing system of rights and duties
is designed to regulate the conflicting purposes of men. An established right is a
promise that a certain kind of behavior will
be backed by the organized force of the state

or at least by the sentiment of the community; a duty is a promise that failure to respect the rights of others in a certain way will be punished. The punishment may be death, imprisonment, loss of property, the nullification of a right, the expression of disapproval. In short, the system of rights and duties is the whole system of promises which the courts and public sentiment will support. It is not a fixed system. It varies from place to place, and from time to time, and with the character of the tribunals and the community. But none the less it makes the conduct of men somewhat rational, and establishes a kind of union in diversity by limiting and defining the freedom with which conflicting purposes can be pursued.

Sometimes the promises are embodied in coercive law: Thou shalt, on penalty of this, do that; thou shalt not do so and so. Sometimes the promise is based on a contract between two parties: there is no obligation to make the contract, but, once made, it must be executed or a certain penalty paid. Sometimes the promise is based on an ecclesiastical code: it must be followed or the wages of sin will be visited either in fact or in anticipation upon the sinner. Sometimes the promise is based on custom: it must be respected or the price of nonconformity, whatever it may happen to be, must be paid. Sometimes the promise is based on habit: it must be executed or the disturbance faced which men feel when they break with their habits.

The question of whether any particular right or duty shall be enforced, the question of how it shall be enforced, whether by the police, by public criticism or private conscience, will not be answered by reasoning *a priori*. It will be answered by the dominant interests in society, each imposing to the limit of its powers the system of rights and duties which most nearly approximates the kind of social harmony it finds convenient and desirable. The system will be a reflection of the power that each interest is able to exert.

The interests which find the rule good will defend it; the interests which find it bad will attack it. Their arguments will be weapons of defense and offense; even the most objective appeal to reason will turn out to be an appeal to desert one cause and enlist in another.

4

In the controversies between interests the question will be raised as to the merits of a particular rule; the argument will turn on whether the rule is good, on whether it should be enforced with this penalty or that. And out of those arguments, by persuasion or coercion, the specific rules of society are made, enforced and revised.

It is the thesis of this book that the members of the public, who are the spectators of action, cannot successfully intervene in a controversy on the merits of the case. They must judge externally, and they can act only by supporting one of the interests directly involved. It

follows that the public interest in a controversy cannot turn upon the specific issue. On
what, then, does it turn? In what phase of
the controversy can the public successfully
interest itself?

Only when somebody objects does the
public know there is a problem; when nobody
any longer objects there is a solution. For
the public, then, any rule is right which is
agreeable to all concerned. It follows that
the public interest in a problem is limited to
this: that there shall be rules, which means
that the rules which prevail shall be enforced,
and that the unenforceable rules shall be
changed according to a settled rule. The
public's opinion that John Smith should or
should not do this or that is immaterial; the
public does not know John Smith's motives
and needs, and is not concerned with them.
But that John Smith shall do what he has
promised to do is a matter of public concern,
for unless the social contracts of men are
made, enforced and revised according to a

settled rule, social organization is impossible. Their conflicting purposes will engender unending problems unless they are regulated by some system of rights and duties.

The interest of the public is not in the rules and contracts and customs themselves but in the maintenance of a régime of rule, contract and custom. The public is interested in law, not in the laws; in the method of law, not in the substance; in the sanctity of contract, not in a particular contract; in understanding based on custom, not in this custom or that. It is concerned in these things to the end that men in their active affairs shall find a *modus vivendi;* its interest is in the workable rule which will define and predict the behavior of men so that they can make their adjustments. The pressure which the public is able to apply through praise and blame, through votes, strikes, boycotts or support can yield results only if it reinforces the men who enforce an old rule or sponsor a new one that is needed.

The public in this theory is not the dispenser of law or morals, but, at best, a reserve force that may be mobilized on behalf of the method and spirit of law and morals. In denying that the public can lay down the rules I have not said that it should abandon any function which the public now exercises. I have merely said that it should abandon a pretense. When the public attempts to deal with the substance it merely becomes the dupe or unconscious ally of a special interest. For there is only one common interest: that all special interests shall act according to settled rule. The moment you ask what rule you invade the realm of competing interests of special points of view, of personal, and class, and sectional, and national bias. The public should not ask what rule because it cannot answer the question. It will contribute its part to the solution of social problems if it recognizes that some system of rights and duties is necessary, but that no particular system is peculiarly sacred.

CHAPTER IX

THE TWO QUESTIONS BEFORE THE PUBLIC

THE multitude of untroubled rules that men live by are of no concern to the public. It has to deal only with the failures. Customs that are accepted by all who are expected to follow them, contracts that are carried out peaceably, promises that are kept, expectations fulfilled, raise no issue. Even when there has been a breach of the rule, there is no public question if the breach is clearly established, the aggression clearly identified, the penalty determined and imposed. The aggressor may be identified because he pleads guilty. He may be identified by some due process though he denies his guilt. The rule, a term under which I mean to include the method of detection, interpretation and enforcement, as well as the precept, is in either case intact. The force of the public can be aligned without hesitation on behalf of the authorities who administer the rule.

There is no question for the public unless there is doubt as to the validity of the rule,—doubt, that is to say, about its meaning, its soundness or the method of its application. When there is doubt the public requires simple, objective tests to help it decide where it will enlist. These tests must, therefore, answer two questions:

First, Is the rule defective?

Second, How shall the agency be recognized which is most likely to mend it?

These are, I should maintain, the only two questions which the public needs to answer in order to exert the greatest influence it is capable of exerting toward the solution of public problems. They are not, please note, the only questions which anybody has to answer to solve a problem. They are the only questions which a member of the public can usefully concern himself with if he wishes to avoid ignorant meddling.

How then shall he know the rule is defective? How shall he recognize the reformer? If he is to answer those questions at all, he must be able to answer them quickly and without real understanding of the problem. Is it possible for him to do that? Can he act intelligently but in ignorance?

I think this apparently paradoxical thing can be done in some such way as the next four chapters describe.

CHAPTER X

THE MAIN VALUE OF PUBLIC DEBATE

THE individual whose action is governed by a rule is interested in its substance. But in those rules which do not control his own action his chief interest is that there should be workable rules.

It follows that the membership of the public is not fixed. It changes with the issue: the actors in one affair are the spectators of another, and men are continually passing back and forth between the field where they are executives and the field where they are members of a public. The distinction between the two is not, as I said in Chapter III, an absolute one: there is a twilight zone where it is hard to say whether a man is acting executively on his opinions or merely acting to influence the opinion of some one else who is acting executively. There is often a mixture of the two types of behavior. And it is this mixture, as well as the lack of a clear line of distinction in all cases, which permits a very large confusion in affairs between a public and a private attitude toward them. The public point of view on a question is muddied by the presence in the public of spurious members, persons who are really acting to bend the rule in their favor while pretending or imagining that they are moved only by the common public need that there shall be an acceptable rule.

At the outset it is important, therefore, to detect and to discount the self-interested group. In saying this I do not mean to cast even the slightest reflection on a union of men to promote their self-interest. It would be futile to do so, because we may take it as certain that men will act to benefit themselves whenever they think they conveniently can. A political theory based on the expectation of self-denial and sacrifice by the run of men in any community would not be worth considering. Nor is it at all evident that the work of the world could be done unless men followed their private interest and contributed to affairs that direct inner knowledge which they thus obtain. Moreover, the adjustments are likely to be much more real if they are made from fully conscious and thoroughly explored special points of view.

Thus the genius of any illuminating public discussion is not to obscure and censor private interest but to help it to sail and to make it sail under its own colors. The true public, in my definition of that term, has to purge itself of the self-interested groups who become confused with it. It must purge itself not because private interests are bad but because private interests cannot successfully be adjusted to each other if any one of them acquires a counterfeit strength. If the true public, concerned only in the fact of adjustment, becomes mobilized behind a private interest seeking to prevail, the adjustment is false; it does not represent the real balance of forces in the affair and the solution will break down. It will break down because the true public will not stay mobilized very long for anything, and when it demobilizes the private interest which was falsely exalted will find its privileges unmanageable. It will be like a man placed on Jack Dempsey's chest by six policemen, and then left there after the policemen have gone home to dinner. It will be like France placed by the Allies upon a prostrate Germany and then left there after the Allies have departed from Europe.

The separation of the public from the self-interested group will not be assisted by the self-interested group. We may be sure that any body of farmers, business men, trade unionists will always call themselves the public if they can. How then is their self-interest to be detected? No ordinary by-stander is equipped to analyze the propaganda by which a private interest seeks to associate itself with the disinterested public. It is a perplexing matter, perhaps the most perplexing in popular government, and the bystander's only recourse is to insist upon debate. He will not be able, we may assume, to judge the merits of the arguments. But if he does insist upon full freedom of discussion, the advocates are very likely to expose one another. Open debate may lead to no conclusion and throw no light whatever on the problem or its answer, but it will tend to betray the partisan and the advocate. And if it has identified them for the true public, debate will have served its main purpose.

The individual not directly concerned may still choose to join the self-interested group and support its cause. But at least he will know that he has made himself a partisan, and thus perhaps he may be somewhat less likely to mistake a party's purpose for the aim of mankind.

Chapter XI

THE DEFECTIVE RULE

I

A MAN violates a rule and then publicly justifies his action. Here in the simplest form is an attack upon the validity of the rule. It is an appeal for a public judgment.

For he claims to have acted under a new rule which is better than the old one. How shall the public decide as between the two? It cannot, we are assuming, enter into the intrinsic merits of the question. It follows that the public must ask the aggressor why he did not first seek the assent of those concerned before he violated the rule. He may say that he did not have time, that he acted in a crisis. In that event, there is no serious question for the public, and his associates will either thank him or call him a fool. But since the circumstances were admittedly exceptional they do not really establish a new rule, and the public may be satisfied if the parties at interest peaceably make the best of the result. But suppose there was no emergency. Suppose the innovator had time to seek assent, but did not on the ground that he knew what was best. He may be fairly condemned; the objections of the other parties may be fairly sustained.

For the right of innovation by fiat cannot be defended as a working principle; a new rule, however excellent in intention, cannot be expected to work unless in some degree it has been first understood and approved by all who must live according to it. The innovator may reply, of course, that he is being condemned by a dogma which is not wholly proved. That may be admitted. Against the principle that a new rule requires assent historic experience can be cited. There have been many instances where a régime has been imposed on an unwilling people and admired later by them for its results. The dogma that assent is necessary is imperfect, as are most principles. But, nevertheless, it is a necessary assumption in society. For if no new rule required assent every one could make his own rule, and there would be no rules. The dogma therefore must be maintained, softened by the knowledge that exceptional times and exceptional men of their own force will make way with any dogma. Since the rules of society cannot be based on exceptions the exceptions must justify themselves.

The test, therefore, of whether a rule has been justifiably broken is the test of assent. The question, then, is how in applying the test of assent a member of the public is to determine whether sufficient assent has been given. How is he to know whether the régime has been imposed by arbitrary force or in substance agreed to?

2

We wish to know if assent is lacking. We know it is lacking because there is open pro-

test. Or we know it because there is a widespread refusal to conform. A workable rule,
which has assent, will not evoke protest or
much disobedience. How shall we, as members of the public, measure the significance of
the protest or the extent of the disobedience?

3

Where very few persons are directly involved in the controversy the public does
best not to intervene at all. One party may
protest, but unless he protests against the
public tribunals set up to adjudicate such
disputes, his protest may be ignored. The
public cannot expect to take part in the
minutiæ of human adjustments however
tragic or important they may be to the individuals concerned. The protest of one
individual against another cannot be treated
as a public matter. Only if the public tribunal is impugned does it become a public
matter, and then only because the case may
require investigation by some other tribunal.

In such disputes the public must trust the agencies of adjustment acting as checks upon each other. When we remember that the public consists of busy men reading newspapers for half an hour or so a day, it is not heartless but merely prudent to deny that it can do detailed justice.

But where many persons are involved in the controversy there is necessarily a public matter. For when many persons are embroiled the effects not only are likely to be wide but there may be need of all the force the public can exert in order to compel a peaceable adjustment.

The public must take account of a protest voiced on behalf of a relatively large number of persons. But how shall the public know that such a protest has been made? It must look to see whether the spokesman is authorized. How shall it tell if he is authorized? How can it tell, that is to say, whether the representative is able to give assent by committing his constituency to a course of action?

Whether the apparent leader is the real leader is a question which the members of a public cannot usually answer directly on the merits. Yet they must answer in some fashion and with some assurance by some rule of thumb.

The rule of thumb is to throw the burden of proof on those who deny that the apparent leader, vested with the external signs of office, is the real leader. As between one nation and another, no matter how obnoxious the other's government may be, if there is no open rebellion, public opinion cannot go behind the returns. For, unless a people is to engage in the hopeless task of playing politics inside another's frontiers, there is no course but to hold that a nation is committed by the officials it fails to discharge. If there is open rebellion, or that milder substitute, an impending election, it may be wise to postpone long term settlements until a firm government has been seated. But settlements, if they are made at all, must be made with the government in office at the other nation's capital.

The same theory holds, with modifications, for large bodies of men within a state. If the officials of the miners' union, for instance, take a position, it is perfectly idle for an employer to deny that they speak for the union miners. He should deny that they speak for the non-union miners, but if the question at issue requires the assent of the union, then, unless the union itself impeaches the leaders, the public must accept them as authorized.

But suppose the leaders are challenged within the union. How shall the importance of the challenge be estimated by the public? Recall that the object is to find out not whether the objectors are right but simply whether the spokesmen can in fact commit their constituents. In weighing the challenge the public's concern is to know how far the opposition can by virtue of its numbers, or of its strategic importance, or its determination, impair the value of an assent. But if we expected the public to make judgments of this sort we should be asking too much of it.

The importance of an opposition can be weighed, if at all, only by rough, external criteria. With an opposition that does not challenge the credentials of the spokesmen, which criticizes but is not in rebellion, the public has no concern. That is an internal affair. It is only an opposition which threatens not to conform that has to be considered.

In such a case, if the spokesmen are elected, they can be held competent to give a reliable assent only until a new election has been held. If the spokesmen are not elective, and a rebellious opposition is evident, their assent can only be taken as tentative. These criteria do not, to be sure, weigh the importance of an opposition, but, by limiting the kind of settlement which can reasonably be made in face of an opposition, they allow for its effect.

They introduce the necessary modification to make workable the general principle that the test of assent by large bodies of men is simply that their spokesmen have agreed.

4

The test of conformity is closely related to the test of assent. For it can be assumed that open criticism of a rule, a custom, a law, an institution, is already accompanied by or will soon be followed by evasion of that rule. It is a fairly safe hypothesis that the run of men wish to conform; that any body of men aroused to the point where they will pay the price of open heresy probably has an arguable case; more certainly that that body will include a considerable number who have passed over the line of criticism into the practice of nonconformity. Their argument may be wrong, the remedy may be foolish, but the fact that they openly criticize at some personal risk is a sign that the rule is not working well. Widespread criticism, therefore, has a significance beyond its intellectual value. It is almost always a symptom on the surface that the rule is unstable.

When a rule is broken not occasionally

but very often the rule is defective. It simply does not define the conduct which normally may be expected of men who live under it. It may sound noble. But it does not work. It does not adjust relations. It does not actually organize society.

In what way the rule is defective the public cannot specifically determine. By the two tests I have suggested, of assent and of conformity, the public can determine the presence of a defect in the rule. But whether that defect is due to a false measure of the changing balance of forces involved, or to neglect of an important interest or some relevant circumstance, or to a bad technic of adjustment, or to contradictions in the rule, or to obscurity, or to lack of machinery for its interpretation or for the deduction of specific rules from general ones, the public cannot judge.

It will have gone, I believe, to the limits of its normal powers if it judges the rule to be defective, and turns then to identify the agency most likely to remedy it.

Chapter XII

THE CRITERIA OF REFORM

I

THE random collections of bystanders who constitute a public could not, even if they had a mind to, intervene in all the problems of the day. They can and must play a part occasionally, I believe, but they cannot take an interest in, they cannot make even the coarsest judgments about, and they will not act even in the most grossly partisan way on, all the questions arising daily in a complex and changing society. Normally they leave their proxies to a kind of professional public consisting of more or less eminent persons. Most issues are never carried beyond this ruling group; the lay publics catch only echoes of the debate.

If, by the push and pull of interested parties and public personages, settlements are made

more or less continually the party in power
has the confidence of the country. In effect,
the outsiders are arrayed behind the dominant
insiders. But if the interested parties cannot
be made to agree, if, as a result, there is disturbance and chronic crisis, then the opposition among the insiders may come to be considered the hope of the country, and be able
to entice the bystanders to its side.

To support the Ins when things are going
well; to support the Outs when they seem
to be going badly, this, in spite of all that has
been said about tweedledum and tweedledee,
is the essence of popular government. Even
the most intelligent large public of which we
have any experience must determine finally
who shall wield the organized power of the
state, its army and its police, by a choice
between the Ins and Outs. A community
where there is no choice does not have popular
government. It is subject to some form
of dictatorship or it is ruled by the intrigues
of the politicians in the lobbies.

Although it is the custom of partisans to speak as if there were radical differences between the Ins and the Outs, it could be demonstrated, I believe, that in stable and mature societies the differences are necessarily not profound. If they were profound, the defeated minority would be constantly on the verge of rebellion. An election would be catastrophic, whereas the assumption in every election is that the victors will do nothing to make life intolerable to the vanquished and that the vanquished will endure with good humor policies which they do not approve.

In the United States, Great Britain, Canada, Australia and in certain of the Continental countries an election rarely means even a fraction of what the campaigners said it would mean. It means some new faces and perhaps a slightly different general tendency in the management of affairs. The Ins may have had a bias toward collectivism; the Outs will lean toward individualism.

The Ins may have been suspicious and non-coöperative in foreign affairs; the Outs will perhaps be more trusting or entertain another set of suspicions. The Ins may have favored certain manufacturing interests; the Outs may favor agricultural interests. But even these differing tendencies are very small as compared with the immense area of agreement, established habit and unavoidable necessity. In fact, one might say that a nation is politically stable when nothing of radical consequence is determined by its elections.

There is, therefore, a certain mock seriousness about the campaigning for votes in well-established communities. Much of the excitement is not about the fate of the nation but simply about the outcome of the game. Some of the excitement is sincere, like any fervor of intoxication. And much of it is deliberately stoked up by the expenditure of money to overcome the inertia of the mass of the voters. For the most part the real difference between the Ins and the Outs is no

more than this: the Ins, after a term of power,
become so committed to policies and so entangled with particular interests that they
lose their neutral freedom of decision. They
cannot then intervene to check the arbitrary
movement of the interests with which they
have become aligned. Then it is time for
the Outs to take power and restore a balance.
The virtue of the Outs in this transaction is
that they are not committed to those particular policies and those particular interests
which have become overweighted.

The test of whether the Ins are handling
affairs effectively is the presence or absence
of disturbing problems. The need of reform
is recognizable, as I pointed out in the chapter
before this one, by the test of assent and the
test of conformity. But it is my opinion that
for the most part the general public cannot
back each reformer on each issue. It must
choose between the Ins and Outs on the basis
of a cumulative judgment as to whether problems are being solved or aggravated. The

particular reformers must look for their support normally to the ruling insiders.

If, however, there is to be any refinement of public opinion it must come from the breaking up of these wholesale judgments into somewhat more retail judgments on the major spectacular issues of the day. Not all of the issues which interest the public are within the scope of politics and reachable through the party system. It seems worth while, therefore, to see whether any canons of judgment can be formulated which could guide the bystanders in particular controversies.

The problem is to locate by clear and coarse objective tests the actor in a controversy who is most worthy of public support.

2

When the rule is plain, its validity unchallenged, the breach clear and the aggressor plainly located, the question does not arise. The public supports the agents of the law, though when the law is working well the support of the public is like the gold reserve of a good bank: it is known to be there and need not be drawn upon. But in many fields of controversy the rule is not plain, or its validity is challenged; each party calls the other aggressor, each claims to be acting for the highest ideals of mankind. In disputes between nations, between sectional interests, between classes, between town and country, between churches, the rules of adjustment are lacking and the argument about them is lost in a fog of propaganda.

Yet it is controversies of this kind, the hardest controversies to disentangle, that the public is called in to judge. Where the facts are most obscure, where precedents are lacking, where novelty and confusion pervade everything, the public in all its unfitness is compelled to make its most important decisions. The hardest problems are those which institutions cannot handle. They are the public's problems.

The one test which the members of a public can apply in these circumstances is to note which party to the dispute is least willing to submit its whole claim to inquiry and to abide by the result. This does not mean that experts are always expert or impartial tribunals really impartial. It means simply that where the public is forced to intervene in a strange and complex affair, the test of public inquiry is the surest clue to the sincerity of the claimant, to his confidence in his ability to stand the ordeal of examination, to his willingness to accept risks for the sake of his faith in the possibility of rational human adjustments. He may impugn a particular tribunal. But he must at least propose another. The test is whether, in the absence of an established rule, he is willing to act according to the forms of law and by a process through which law may be made.

Of all the tests which public opinion can employ, the test of inquiry is the most generally useful. If the parties are willing to accept it, there is at once an atmosphere of reason. There is prospect of a settlement. Failing that there is at least a delay of summary action and an opportunity for the clarification of issues. And failing that there is a high probability that the most arbitrary of the disputants will be isolated and clearly identified. It is no wonder that this is the principle invoked for the so-called nonjusticiable questions in all the recent experiments under the covenant of the League of Nations [1] and the Protocol for the Pacific Settlement of International Disputes.[2] For in applying this test of inquiry, what we affirm is this: That there is a dispute. That the merits are not clear. That the policy which ought to be applied is not established. That, nevertheless, we of the public outside say that those who are quarreling must act as if there were law to cover the case. That,

[1] Articles XIII, XV.
[2] Articles 4, 5, 6, 7, 8, 10.

even if the material for a reasoned conclusion is lacking, we demand the method and spirit of reason. That we demand any sacrifice that may be necessary, the postponment of satisfaction of their just needs, the risk that one of them will be defeated and that an injustice will be done. These things we affirm because we are maintaining a society based on the principle that all controversies are soluble by peaceable agreement.

They may not be. But on that dogma our society is founded. And that dogma we are compelled to defend. We can defend it, too, with a good enough conscience, however disconcerting some of its immediate consequences may be. For, by insisting in all disputes upon the spirit of reason, we shall tend in the long run to confirm the habit of reason. And where that habit prevails no point of view can seem absolute to him who holds it, and no problem between men so difficult that there is not at least a *modus vivendi*.

The test of inquiry is the master test by which the public can use its force to extend the frontiers of reason.

3

But while the test of inquiry may distinguish the party which is entitled to initial support, it is of value only where one party refuses inquiry. If all submit to inquiry, it reveals nothing. And in any event it reveals nothing about the prospects of the solution proposed. The party seeking publicity may have less to conceal, and may mean well, but sincerity unfortunately is no index of intelligence. By what criteria are the public then to judge the new rule which is proposed as a solution?

The public cannot tell whether the new rule will, in fact, work. It may assume, however, that in a changing world no rule will always work. A rule, therefore, should be organized so that experience will clearly reveal its defects. The rule should be so clear that a violation is apparent. But since no generality can cover all cases, this means simply that the rule must contain a settled procedure by which it can be interpreted. Thus a treaty which says that a certain territory shall be evacuated when certain conditions are fulfilled is quite defective, and should be condemned, if it does not provide a way of defining exactly what those conditions are and when they have been fulfilled. A rule, in other words, must include the means of its own clarification, so that a breach shall be undeniably overt. Then only does it take account of experience which no human intelligence can foresee.

It follows from this that a rule must be organized so that it can be amended without revolution. Revision must be possible by consent. But assent is not always given, even when the arguments in favor of a change are overwhelming. Men will stand on what they call their rights. Therefore, in order that deadlock should be dissoluble, a rule should provide that subject to a certain formal procedure the controversy over revision shall be public. This will often break up the obstruction. Where it does not, the community is pretty certain to become engaged on behalf of one of the partisans. This is likely to be inconvenient to all concerned, and the inconvenience due to meddling in the substance of a controversy by a crude, violent and badly aimed public opinion at least may teach those directly concerned not to invoke interference the next time.

But although amendment should be possible, it should not be continual or unforeseen. There should be time for habit and custom to form. The pot should not be made to boil all the time, or be stirred up for some comparatively insignificant reason, whenever an orator sees a chance to make himself important. Since the habits and expectations of many different persons are involved in an institution, some way must be found of giving it stability without freezing it *in statu quo*. This can be done by requiring that amendment shall be in order only after due notice.

What due notice may be in each particular case, the public cannot say. Only the parties at interest are likely to know where the rhythm of their affairs can be interrupted most conveniently. Due notice will be one period of time for men operating on long commitments and another for men operating on short ones. But the public can watch to see whether the principle of due notice is embodied in the proposed settlement.

To judge a new rule, then, the tests proposed here are three: Does it provide for its own clarification? for its own amendment by consent? for due notice that amendment will be proposed? The tests are designed for use in judging the prospects of a settlement not by its substance but by its procedure. A reform which satisfies these tests is normally entitled to public support.

4

This is as far as I know how at present to work out an answer to the question which we inherit from Aristotle: can simple criteria be formulated which will show the bystander where to align himself in complex affairs?

I have suggested that the main value of debate is not that it reveals the truth about the controversy to the audience but that it may identify the partisans. I have suggested further that a problem exists where a rule of action is defective, and that its defectiveness can best be judged by the public through the test of assent and the test of conformity. For remedies I have assumed that normally the public must turn to the Outs as against the Ins, although these wholesale judgments may be refined by more analytical tests for specific issues. As samples of these more analytical tests I have suggested the test of inquiry for confused controversies, and for reforms the test of interpretation, of amendment and of due notice.

These criteria are neither exhaustive nor definitive. Yet, however much tests of this character are improved by practice and reflection, it seems to me there always must remain many public affairs to which they cannot be applied. I do not believe that the public can intervene successfully in all public questions. Many problems cannot be advanced by that obtuse partisanship which is fundamentally all that the public can bring to bear upon them. There is no reason to be surprised, therefore, if the tests I have outlined, or any others that are a vast improvement upon them, are not readily applicable to all questions that are raised in the discussions of the day.

I should simply maintain that where the members of a public cannot use tests of this sort as a guide to action, the wisest course for them is not to act at all. They had better be neutral, if they can restrain themselves, than blindly partisan. For where events are so confused or so subtly balanced or so hard to understand that they do not yield to judgments of the kind I have been outlining here, the probabilities are very great that the public can produce only muddle if it meddles. For not all problems are soluble in the present state of human knowledge. Many which may be soluble are not soluble with any force the public can exert. Some time alone will cure, and some are the fate of man. It is not essential, therefore, always to do something.

It follows that the proper limits of intervention by the public in affairs are determined by its capacity to make judgments. These limits may be extended as new and better criteria are formulated, or as men become more expert through practice. But where there are no tests, where such tests as these cannot be used, where, in other words, only an opinion on the actual merits of the dispute itself would be of any use, any positive action the bystanders are likely to take is almost certain to be more of a nuisance than a benefit. Their duty is to keep an open mind and wait to see. The existence of a usable test is itself the test of whether the public ought to intervene.

Chapter XIII

THE PRINCIPLES OF PUBLIC OPINION

I

THE tests outlined in the preceding chapters have certain common characteristics. They all select a few samples of behavior or a few aspects of a proposal. They measure these samples by rough but objective, by highly generalized but definite standards. And they yield a judgment which is to justify the public in aligning itself for or against certain actors in the matter at issue.

I do not, of course, set great store upon my formulation of these tests. That is wholly tentative, being put out merely as a basis of discussion and to demonstrate that the formulation of tests suited to the nature of public opinion is not impracticable. But I do attach great importance to the character of these tests.

The principles underlying them are these:

1. Executive action is not for the public. The public acts only by aligning itself as the partisan of some one in a position to act executively.

2. The intrinsic merits of a question are not for the public. The public intervenes from the outside upon the work of the insiders.

3. The anticipation, the analysis and the solution of a question are not for the public. The public's judgment rests on a small sample of the facts at issue.

4. The specific, technical, intimate criteria required in the handling of a question are not for the public. The public's criteria are generalized for many problems; they turn essentially on procedure and the overt, external forms of behavior.

5. What is left for the public is a judgment as to whether the actors in the controversy are following a settled rule of behavior or their own arbitrary desires. This judgment

must be made by sampling an external aspect of the behavior of the insiders.

6. In order that this sampling shall be pertinent, it is necessary to discover criteria, suitable to the nature of public opinion, which can be relied upon to distinguish between reasonable and arbitrary behavior.

7. For the purposes of social action, reasonable behavior is conduct which follows a settled course whether in making a rule, in enforcing it or in amending it.

It is the task of the political scientist to devise the methods of sampling and to define the criteria of judgment. It is the task of civic education in a democracy to train the public in the use of these methods. It is the task of those who build institutions to take them into account.

2

These principles differ radically from those on which democratic reformers have proceeded. At the root of the effort to educate a people for self-government there has, I believe, always been the assumption that the voter should aim to approximate as nearly as he can the knowledge and the point of view of the responsible man. He did not, of course, in the mass, ever approximate it very nearly. But he was supposed to. It was believed that if only he could be taught more facts, if only he would take more interest, if only he would read more and better newspapers, if only he would listen to more lectures and read more reports, he would gradually be trained to direct public affairs. The whole assumption is false. It rests upon a false conception of public opinion and a false conception of the way the public acts. No sound scheme of civic education can come of it. No progress can be made toward this unattainable ideal.

This democratic conception is false because it fails to note the radical difference between the experience of the insider and the outsider; it is fundamentally askew because it asks the outsider to deal as successfully with the substance of a question as the insider. He cannot do it. No scheme of education can equip him in advance for all the problems of mankind; no device of publicity, no machinery of enlightenment, can endow him during a crisis with the antecedent detailed and technical knowledge which is required for executive action.

The democratic ideal has never defined the function of the public. It has treated the public as an immature, shadowy executive of all things. The confusion is deep-seated in a mystical notion of society. "The people" were regarded as a person; their wills as a will; their ideas as a mind; their mass as an organism with an organic unity of which the individual was a cell. Thus the voter identified himself with the officials. He tried to think that their thoughts were his thoughts, that their deeds were his deeds, and even that in some mysterious way they were a part of him. All this confusion of identities led naturally to the theory that everybody was doing everything. It prevented democracy from arriving at a clear idea of its own limits and attainable ends. It obscured for the purposes of government and social education the separation of function and the specialization in training which have gradually been established in most human activities.

Democracy, therefore, has never developed an education for the public. It has merely given it a smattering of the kind of knowledge which the responsible man requires. It has, in fact, aimed not at making good citizens but at making a mass of amateur executives. It has not taught the child how to act as a member of the public. It has merely given him a hasty, incomplete taste of what he might have to know if he meddled in everything. The result is a bewildered public and a mass of insufficiently trained officials. The responsible men have obtained their training not from the courses in "civics" but in the law schools and law offices and in business. The public at large, which includes everybody outside the field of his own responsible knowledge, has had no coherent political training of any kind. Our civic education does not even begin to tell the voter how he can reduce the maze of public affairs to some intelligible form.

Critics have not been lacking, of course, who pointed out what a hash democracy was making of its pretensions to government. These critics have seen that the important decisions were taken by individuals, and that public opinion was uninformed, irrelevant and meddlesome. They have usually concluded that there was a congenital difference between the masterful few and the ignorant many. They are the victims of a superficial analysis of the evils they see so clearly.

The fundamental difference which matters is that between insiders and outsiders. Their relations to a problem are radically different. Only the insider can make decisions, not because he is inherently a better man but because he is so placed that he can understand and can act. The outsider is necessarily ignorant, usually irrelevant and often meddlesome, because he is trying to navigate the ship from dry land. That is why excellent automobile manufacturers, literary critics and scientists often talk such nonsense about politics. Their congenital excellence, if it exists, reveals itself only in their own activity. The aristocratic theorists work from the fallacy of supposing that a sufficiently excellent square peg will also fit a round hole. In short, like the democratic theorists, they miss the essence of the matter, which is, that competence exists only in relation to function; that men are not good, but good for something; that men cannot be educated, but only educated for something.

Education for citizenship, for membership in the public, ought, therefore, to be distinct from education for public office. Citizenship involves a radically different relation to affairs, requires different intellectual habits and different methods of action. The force of public opinion is partisan, spasmodic, simple-minded and external. It needs for its direction, as I have tried to show in these chapters, a new intellectual method which shall provide it with its own usable canons of judgment.

PART III

Chapter XIV

SOCIETY IN ITS PLACE

I

A FALSE ideal of democracy can lead only to disillusionment and to meddlesome tyranny. If democracy cannot direct affairs, then a philosophy which expects it to direct them will encourage the people to attempt the impossible; they will fail, but that will interfere outrageously with the productive liberties of the individual. The public must be put in its place, so that it may exercise its own powers, but no less and perhaps even more, so that each of us may live free of the trampling and the roar of a bewildered herd.

2

The source of that bewilderment lies, I think, in the attempt to ascribe organic unity and purpose to society. We have been taught to think of society as a body, with a mind, a soul and a purpose, not as a collection of men, women and children whose minds, souls and purposes are variously related. Instead of being allowed to think realistically of a complex of social *relations*, we have had foisted upon us by various great propagative movements the notion of a mythical entity, called Society, the Nation, the Community.

In the course of the nineteenth century society was personified under the influence largely of the nationalist and the socialist movements. Each of these doctrinal influences in its own way insisted upon treating the public as the agent of an overmastering social purpose. In point of fact, the real agents were the nationalist leaders and their lieutenants, the social reformers and their lieutenants. But they moved behind a veil of imagery. And the public was habituated to think that any one conforming to the sterotype of nationalism or of social welfare was entitled to support. What the nationalist rulers thought and did was the nation's purpose, and the touchstone for all patriots; what the reformers proposed was the benevolent consciousness of the human race moving mysteriously but progressively toward perfection.

The deception was so generally practised that it was often practised sincerely. But to maintain the fiction that their purposes were the spirit of mankind, public men had to accustom themselves to telling the public only a part of what they told themselves. And, incidentally, they confessed to themselves only a part of the truth on which they were acting. Candor in public life became a question of policy and not a rule of life.

"He may judge rightly," Mr. Keynes once said of Mr. Lloyd George,[1] "that this is the best of which a democracy is capable,— to be jockeyed, humbugged, cajoled along the right road. A prejudice for truth or for

[1] John Maynard Keynes, *A Revision of the Treaty*, p. 4.

sincerity as a method may be a prejudice based on some æsthetic or personal standard inconsistent, in politics, with practical good. We cannot yet tell."

We do know, as a matter of experience, that all the cards are not laid face up upon the table. For however deep the personal prejudice of the statesman in favor of truth as a method, he is almost certainly forced to treat truth as an element of policy. The evidence on this point is overwhelming. No statesman risks the safety of an army out of sheer devotion to truth. He does not endanger a diplomatic negotiation in order to enlighten everybody. He does not usually forfeit his advantages in an election in order to speak plainly. He does not admit his own mistakes because confession is so good for the soul. In so far as he has power to control the publication of truth, he manipulates it to what he considers the necessities of action, of bargaining, morale and prestige. He may misjudge the necessities. He may exaggerate the goodness of his aims. But where there is a purpose in public affairs there are also apparent necessities which weigh in the balance against the indiscreet expression of belief. The public man does not and cannot act on the fiction that his mind is also the public mind.

You cannot account for this, as angry democrats have done by dismissing all public men as dishonest. It is not a question of personal morals. The business man, the trade-union leader, the college president, the minister of religion, the editor, the critic and the prophet, all feel as Jefferson did when he wrote that "although we often wished to go faster we slackened our pace that our less ardent colleagues might keep pace with us . . . [and] by this harmony of the bold with the cautious, we advanced with our constituents in undivided mass." [2]

The necessity for an "undivided mass" makes men put truth in the second place.

[2] In a letter to William Wirt, cited by John Sharp Williams, *Thomas Jefferson*, p. 7.

I do not wish to argue that the necessity is not often a real one. When a statesman tells me that it is not safe for him to disclose all the facts, I am content to trust him in this if I trust him at all. There is nothing misleading in a frank refusal to tell. The mischief comes in the pretense that all is being told, that the public is entirely in the confidence of the public man. And that mischief has its source in the sophistry that the public and all the individuals composing it are one mind, one soul, one purpose. It is seen to be an absurd sophistry, once we look it straight in the face. It is an unnecessary sophistry. For we do well enough with doctors, though we are ignorant of medicine, and with engine drivers, though we cannot drive a locomotive; why not, then, with a Senator, though we cannot pass an examination on the merits of an agricultural bill?

Yet we are so deeply indoctrinated with the notion of union based upon identity, that we are most reluctant to admit that there is room in the world for different and more or less separate purposes. The monistic theory has an air of great stability about it; we are afraid if we do not hang together we shall all hang separately. The pluralistic theory, as its leading advocate, Mr. Laski, has pointed out, seems to carry with it "a hint of anarchy." [3] Yet the suggestion is grossly exaggerated. There is least anarchy precisely in those areas of society where separate functions are most clearly defined and brought into orderly adjustment; there is most anarchy in those twilight zones between nations, between employers and employees, between sections and classes and races, where nothing is clearly defined, where separateness of purpose is covered up and confused, where false unities are worshiped, and each special interest is forever proclaiming itself the voice of the people and attempting to impose its purpose upon everybody as the purpose of all mankind.

[3] Harold J. Laski, *Studies in the Problem of Sovereignty*, p. 24.

3

To this confusion liberalism has with the kindest intentions contributed greatly. Its main insight was into the prejudices of the individual; the liberal discovered a method of proving that men are finite, that they cannot escape from the flesh. From the so-called age of enlightenment down to our day the heavy guns of criticism have been used to make men realize that they submit, as Bacon said, the shadows of things to the desires of the mind. Once the resistance was broken by proof that man belonged to the natural world, his pretensions to absolute certainty were attacked from every quarter. He was shown the history of his ideas and of his customs, and he was driven to acknowledge that they were bounded by time and space and circumstance. He was shown that there is a bias in all opinion, even in opinion purged of desire, for the man who holds the opinion must stand at some point in space and time and can see not the whole world but only the world as seen from that point. So men learned that they saw a little through their own eyes, and much more through reports of what other men thought they had seen. They were made to understand that all human eyes have habits of vision, which are often stereotyped, which always throw facts into a perspective; and that the whole of experience is more sophisticated than the naïve mind suspects. For its pictures of the world are drawn from things half heard and of things half seen; they deal with the shadows of things unsteadily, and submit unconsciously to the desires of the mind.

It was an amazing and unsettling revelation, and liberalism never quite knew what to do with it. In a theater in Moscow a certain M. Yevreynoff carried the revelation to one of its logical conclusions. He produced the monodrama.[4] This is a play in which

[4] Kenneth Macgowan, *The Theatre of Tomorrow*, pp. 249-50.

the action, the setting and all the characters
are seen by the audience through the eyes
of one character only, as the hero sees them,
and they take on the quality which his mind
imagines they possess. Thus in the old
theater, if the hero drank too much, he
reeled in the midst of a sober environment.
But in M. Yevreynoff's supremely liberal
theater, if I understand Mr. Macgowan's
account of it correctly, the drunkard will
not reel about the lamppost; two lampposts
will reel about him, and he will be dressed,
because that is the way he feels, like Napoleon
Bonaparte.

M. Yevreynoff has troubled me a good deal,
for he seemed to have finished off the liberal
with a fool's cap, and left him sitting in a
world that does not exist, except as so many
crazy mirrors reflecting his own follies one
upon the other. But then I recalled that M.
Yevreynoff's logic was defective and make-
believe. He had all the time stood soberly
outside his own drunken hero, and so had his

audience; the universe had not after all gone up in the smoke of one fantasy; the drunken hero had his point of view, but, after all, there were others, just as authentic, with which in the course of his career he might collide. There might be a policeman, for example, with fantasies to be sure, but his own, who would break in upon the monodrama and remind the hero, and us, that when we submit the shadows of things to the desires of the mind we do not submit the things themselves.

But while all this does vindicate the sanity of the liberal criticism, it does not answer the question: since every action has to be taken by somebody, since everybody is in some degree a drunken hero with two lampposts teetering about him, how can any common good be furthered by this creature who is dominated by his special purposes? The answer was that it could be furthered by taming his purposes, enlightening them and fitting them into each other as the violin and the drum are fitted together into the orchestra. The answer was not acceptable in the nineteenth century, when men, in spite of all their iconoclasm, were still haunted by the phantom of identity. So liberals refused to write harmonious but separate parts for the violinist and the drummer. They made, instead, a noble appeal to their highest instincts. They spoke over the heads of men to man.

These general appeals were as vague as they were broad. They gave particular men no clue as to how to behave sincerely, but they furnished them with an excellent masquerade when they behaved arbitrarily. Thus the trappings of liberalism came into the service of commercial exploiters, of profiteers and prohibitionists and jingoes, of charlatans and the makers of buncombe.

For liberalism had burned down the barn to roast the pig. The discovery of prejudice in all particular men gave the liberal a shock from which he never recovered. He was so utterly disconcerted by his own discovery of a necessary but perfectly obvious truth, that he took flight into generalities. The appeal to everybody's conscience gave nobody a clue how to act; the voter, the politician, the laborer, the capitalist had to construct their own codes *ad hoc*, accompanied perhaps by an expansive liberal sentiment, but without intellectual guidance from liberal thought. In time, when liberalism had lost its accidental association with free trade and *laissez faire*, through their abandonment in practice, it sadly justified itself as a necessary and useful spirit, as a kind of genial spook worth having around the place. For when individual men, guided by no philosophy but their own temporary rationalizations, got themselves embroiled, the spook would appear and in a peroration straighten out the more arbitrary biases they displayed.

Yet even in this disembodied state liberalism is important. It tends to awaken a milder spirit; it softens the hardness of action. But it does not dominate action, because it has eliminated the actor from its scheme of things. It cannot say: You do this and you do that, as all ruling philosophies must. It can only say: That is n't fair, that's selfish, that's tyrannical. Liberalism has been, therefore, a defender of the under dog, and his liberator, but not his guide, when he is free. Top dog himself, he easily leaves his liberalism aside, and to liberals the sour reflection that they have forged a weapon of release but not a way of life.

The liberals have misunderstood the nature of the public to which they appealed. The public in any situation is, in fact, merely those persons, indirectly concerned, who might align themselves in support of one of the actors. But the liberal took no such uninflated view of the public. He assumed that all mankind was within hearing, that all mankind when it heard would respond homogeneously because it had a single soul. His appeal to this cosmopolitan, universal, disinterested intuition in everybody was equivalent to an appeal to nobody.

No such fallacy is to be found in the political philosophies which active men have lived by. They have all assumed, as a matter of course, that in the struggle against evil it was necessary to call upon some specific agent to do the work. Even when the thinker was out of temper with the human race, he had always hitherto made somebody the hero of his campaign. It was the peculiarity of liberalism among theories which have played a great part in the world that it attempted to eliminate the hero entirely.

Plato would certainly have thought this strange: his *Republic* is a tract on the proper education of a ruling class. Dante, in the turmoil of thirteenth century Florence, seeking order and stability, addressed himself not to the conscience of Christendom but to the Imperial Party. The great state builders of modern times, Hamilton, Cavour, Bismarck, Lenin, each had in mind somebody, some group of real people, who were to realize his program. The agents in the theory have varied, of course; here they are the landlords, then the peasants, or the unions, or the military class, or the manufacturers; there are theories addressed to a church, to the ruling classes in particular nations, to some nation or race. The theories are always, except in the liberal philosophy, addressed to somebody.

By comparison the liberal philosophy has an air of vague unworldiness. Yet the regard of men for it has been persistent; somehow or other with all the lapses in its logic and with all its practical weaknesses it touches a human need. These appeals from men to man: are they not a way of saying that men desire peace, that there is a harmony attainable in which all men can live and let live? It seems so to me. The attempt to escape from particular purposes into some universal purpose, from personality into something impersonal, is, to be sure, a flight from

the human problem, but it is at the same time
a demonstration of how we wish to see that
problem solved. We seek an adjustment, as
perfect as possible, as untroubled as it was
before we were born. Even if man were a
fighting animal, as some say he is, he would
wish for a world in which he could fight perfectly, with enemies fleet enough to extend
him and not too fleet to elude him. All men
desire their own perfect adjustment, but they
desire it, being finite men, on their own terms.

Because liberalism could not accommodate
the universal need of adjustment to the per-
manence and the reality of individual purpose, it remained an incomplete, a disembodied philosophy. It was frustrated over
the ancient problem of the One and the Many.
Yet the problem is not so insoluble once we
cease to personify society. It is only when we
are compelled to personify society that we are
puzzled as to how many separate organic
individuals can be united in one homogeneous
organic individual. This logical underbrush

is cleared away if we think of society not as the name of a thing but as the name of all the adjustments between individuals and their things.   Then, we can say without theoretical qualms what common sense plainly tells us is so: it is the individuals who act, not society; it is the individuals who think, not the collective mind; it is the painters who paint, not the artistic spirit of the age; it is the soldiers who fight and are killed, not the nation; it is the merchant who exports, not the country.   It is their relations with each other that constitute a society.   And it is about the ordering of those relations that the individuals not executively concerned in a specific disorder may have public opinions and may intervene as a public.

Chapter XV

ABSENTEE RULERS

I

THE practical effect of the monistic theories of society has been to rationalize that vast concentrating of political and economic power in the midst of which we live. Since society was supposed to have organic purposes of its own, it came to seem quite reasonable that these purposes should be made manifest to a people by laws and decisions from a central point. Somebody had to have a purpose revealed to him which could be treated as the common purpose; if it was to be accepted it had to be enforced by command; if it was really to look like the national purpose, it had to be handed down as a rule binding upon all. Thus men could say with Goethe:

"And then a mighty work completed stands,
One mind suffices for a thousand hands." [1]

[1] *Faust*, Part II, Act v, scene 3.

In this fashion the eulogies of the Great Society have been made. Two thousand years ago it was possible for whole civilizations as mature as the Chinese and the Greco-Roman to coexist in total indifference to one another. Today the food supplies, the raw materials, the manufactures, the communications and the peace of the world constitute one great system which cannot be thrown severely out of balance in any part without disturbing the whole.

Looked at from the top, the system in its far-flung and intricate adjustments has a certain grandeur. It might, as some hopeful persons think, even ultimately mean the brotherhood of man since all men living in advanced communities are now in quite obvious fashion dependent upon one another. But the individual man cannot look at the system steadily from the top or see it in its ultimate speculative possibilities. For him it means in practice, along with the rise in certain of his material standards of life, a nerve-wracking increase of the incalculable forces that bear upon his fate. My neighbor in the country who borrowed money to raise potatoes which he cannot sell for cash looks at the bills from the village store asking for immediate cash payments, and does not share the philosophic hopeful view of the interdependence of the world. When unseen commission merchants in New York City refuse his potatoes, the calamity is as dumfounding as a drought or a plague of locusts.

The harvest in September of the planting in May is now determined not only by wind and weather, which his religion has from time immemorial justified, but by a tangle of distant human arrangements of which only loose threads are in his hands. He may live more richly than his ancestors; he may be wealthier and healthier and, for all he knows, even happier. But he gambles with the behavior of unseen men in a bewildering way. His relations with invisibly managed markets are decisively important for him; his own foresight is not dependable. He is a link in a chain that stretches beyond his horizon.

The rôle that salesmanship and speculation play is a measure of the spread between the work men do and the results. To market the output of Lancashire, says Dibblee,[2] "the merchants and warehousemen of Manchester and Liverpool, not to mention the marketing organizations in other Lancashire towns, have a greater capital employed than that required in all the manufacturing industries of the cotton trade." And, according to Anderson's calculations,[3] the grain received at Chicago in 1915 was sold sixty-two times in futures, as well as an unknown number of times in spot transactions. Where men produce for invisible and uncertain markets "the initial plans of enterprisers"[4] cannot be adequate. The adjustments, often very crude and costly, are effected by salesmanship and speculation.

[2] Dibblee, *The Laws of Supply and Demand*, cited by B. M. Anderson, Jr., *The Value of Money*, p. 259.

[3] B. M. Anderson, Jr., *The Value of Money*, p. 251.

[4] *Ibid.*

Under these conditions neither the discipline of the craftsman who controls his process from beginning to end nor the virtues of thrift, economy and work are a complete guide to a successful career. Defoe in his *Complete English Tradesman* [5] could say that "trade is not a ball where people appear in masque and act a part to make sport . . . but is a plain, visible scene of honest life . . . supported by prudence and frugality" . . . and so "prudent management and frugality will increase any fortune to any degree." Benjamin Franklin might opine that "he that gets all he can honestly, and saves all he gets (necessary expenses excepted) will certainly become rich, if that Being who governs the world, to whom all should look for a blessing on their honest endeavors, doth not in His wise providence, otherwise determine." Young men were until quite recently exhorted in the very words of Defoe and Franklin, though Franklin's rather

[5] *Cf.* Werner Lombart, *The Quintessence of Capitalism*, Chapter VII.

canny allowance for the whims of the Almighty was not always included. But of late the gospel of success contains less about frugality and more about visions and the message of business. This new gospel, beneath all its highfalutin cant, points dimly though excitedly to the truth that for business success a man must project his mind over an invisible environment.

This need has bred an imperious tendency to organization on a large scale. To defend themselves against the economic powers of darkness, against great monopolies or a devastating competition, the farmers set up great centralized selling agencies. Business men form great trade associations. Everybody organizes, until the number of committees and their paid secretaries cannot be computed. The tendency is pervasive. We have had, if I remember correctly, National Smile Week. At any rate we have had Nebraska which discovered that if you wish to prohibit liquor in Nebraska you must prohibit it

everywhere. Nebraska cannot live by itself
alone, being too weak to control an international traffic. We have had the socialist
who was convinced that socialism can maintain itself only on a socialist planet. We have
had Secretary Hughes who was convinced
that capitalism could exist only on a capitalist
planet. We have had all the imperialists who
could not live unless they advanced the back-
ward races. And we have had the Ku Klux
Klansmen who were persuaded that if you organized and sold hate on a country-wide scale
there would be lots more hate than there was
before. We have had the Germans before 1914
who were told they had to choose between
"world power or downfall," and the French for
some years after 1919 who could not be
"secure" in Europe unless every one else was
insecure. We have had all conceivable manifestations of the impulse to seek stability in an
incalculable environment by standardizing for
one's own apparent convenience all those who
form the context of one's activity.

It has entailed perpetual effort to bring more and more men under the same law and custom, and then, of course, to assume control of the lawmaking and law-enforcing machinery in this larger area. The effect has been to concentrate decision in central governments, in distant executive offices, in caucuses and in steering committees. Whether this concentration of power is good or bad, permanent or passing, this at least is certain. The men who make the decisions at these central points are remote from the men they govern and the facts with which they deal. Even if they conscientiously regard themselves as agents or trustees, it is a pure fiction to say that they are carrying out the will of the people. They may govern the people wisely. They are not governing with the active consultation of the people. They can at best lay down policy wholesale in response to electorates which judge and act upon only a detail of the result. For the governors see a kind of whole which obscures the infinite varieties of particular interests; their vices are abstraction and generalization which appear in politics as legalism and bureaucracy. The governed, on the contrary, see vivid aspects of a whole which they can rarely imagine, and their prevailing vice is to mistake a local prejudice for a universal truth.

The widening distance between the centers where decisions are taken and the places where the main work of the world is done has undermined the discipline of public opinion upon which all the earlier theorists relied.[6] A century ago the model of popular government was the self-sufficing township in which the voters' opinions were formed and corrected by talk with their neighbors. They might entertain queer opinions about witches and spirits and foreign peoples and other worlds. But about the village itself the facts were not radically in dispute, and nothing was likely to happen that the elders could not with a

[6] *Cf.* my *Public Opinion*, Chapters XVI and XVII.

little ingenuity bring under a well-known
precedent of their common law.

But under absentee government these
checks upon opinion are lacking. The consequences are often so remote and long de-
layed that error is not promptly disclosed.
The conditioning factors are distant; they do
not count vividly in our judgments. The
reality is inaccessible; the bounds of sub-
jective opinion are wide. In the interdepend-
ent world, desire, rather than custom or objective law, tends to become the criterion of
men's conduct. They formulate their demands at large for "security" at the expense
of every one else's safety, for "morality" at
the expense of other men's tastes and comfort,
for the fulfillment of a national destiny that
consists in taking what you want when you
want it. The lengthening of the interval
between conduct and experience, between
cause and effect, has nurtured a cult of self-
expression in which each thinker thinks about
his own thoughts and has subtle feelings about

his feelings. That he does not in consequence deeply affect the course of affairs is not surprising.

2

The centralizing tendencies of the Great Society have not been accepted without protest, and the case against them has been stated again and again.[7] Without local institutions, said de Tocqueville, a nation may give itself a free government, but it does not possess the spirit of liberty. To concentrate power at one point is to facilitate the seizure of power. "What are you going to do?" Arthur Young asked some provincials at the time of the French Revolution. "We do not know," they replied; "we must see what Paris is going to do." Local interests handled from a distant central point are roughly handled by busy and inattentive men. And in the meantime the local training

[7] In a convenient form by J. Charles Brun, *Le Régionalisme*, pp. 13 *et seq.* Cf. also Walter Thompson, *Federal Centralization*, Chapter XIX.

and the local winnowing of political talent are
neglected. The overburdened central authority expands into a vast hierarchy of bureau-
crats and clerks manipulating immense stacks
of paper, always dealing with symbols on
paper, rarely with things or with people. The
genius of centralization reached its climax
in the famous boast of a French minister of
education, who said: It is three o'clock; all
the pupils in the third grade throughout
France are now composing a Latin verse.

There is no need to labor the point. The
more centralization the less can the people
concerned be consulted and give conscious
assent. The more extensive the rule laid
down the less account it can take of fact and
special circumstance. The more it conflicts
with local experience, the more distant its
source and wholesale its character, the less
easily enforceable it is. General rules will
tend to violate particular needs. Distantly
imposed rules usually lack the sanction of
consent. Being less suited to the needs of

men, and more external to their minds, they rest on force rather than on custom and on reason.

A centralized society dominated by the fiction that the governors are the spokesmen of a common will tends not only to degrade initiative in the individual but to reduce to insignificance the play of public opinion. For when the action of a whole people is concentrated, the public is so vast that even the crude objective judgments it might make on specific issues cease to be practicable. The tests indicated in preceding chapters by which a public might judge the workability of a rule or the soundness of a new proposal have little value when the public runs into millions and the issues are hopelessly entangled with each other. It is idle under such circumstances to talk about democracy, or about the refinement of public opinion. With such monstrous complications the public can do little more than at intervals to align itself heavily for or against the régime in power, and for the rest to bear with its works, obeying meekly or evading, as seems most convenient. For, in practice, the organic theory of society means a concentration of power; that is, the way the notion of one purpose is actually embodied in affairs. And this in turn means that men must either accept frustration of their own purposes or contrive somehow to frustrate that declared purpose of that central power which pretends it is the purpose of all.

Chapter XVI

THE REALMS OF DISORDER

I

YET the practice of centralization and the philosophy which personifies society have acquired a great hold upon men. The dangers are well known. If, nevertheless, the practice and the theory persist, it cannot be merely because men have been led astray by false doctrine.

If you examine the difficulties enumerated by the sponsors of great centralizing measures, such as national prohibition, the national child labor amendment, federal control of education or the nationalization of railroads, they are reducible, I think, to one dominating idea: that it is necessary to extend the area of control over all the factors in a problem or the problem will be insoluble anywhere.

It was to this idea that Mr. Lloyd George appealed when he faced his critics at the end of his administration. While his words are the words of a skilful debater, the idea behind them might almost be called the supreme motive of all the imperial and centralizing tendencies of the Great Society:

"Lord Grey sought to make peace in the Balkans. He made peace. That peace did not stand the jolting of the train that carried it from London to the Balkans. It fell to pieces before it ever reached Sofia. That was not his fault. The plan was good. The intentions were excellent. *But there were factors there which he could not control.* He tried to prevent the Turks from entering the war against us, a most important matter. German diplomacy was too strong for him. He tried to prevent Bulgaria from entering the war against us. There again German diplomacy defeated us. Well, now I have never taunted Lord Grey with that. I do not taunt him now, but what I say is that when you get into the realm of foreign affairs there are things I will not say you cannot visualize, because you do, but there are factors you cannot influence." [1]

Mr. Lloyd George might have said the same of domestic affairs. There, too, factors abound which you cannot influence. And as empires expand to protect their frontiers, and then expand further to protect the protections to their frontiers, so central governments have been led step by step to take one interest after another under their control.

2

For the democracies are haunted by this dilemma: they are frustrated unless in the laying down of rules there is a large measure of assent; yet they seem unable to find solutions of their greatest problems except through centralized governing by means of extensive rules which necessarily ignore the principle of assent. The problems that vex democracy

[1] Speech at Manchester, October 14, 1922.

seem to be unmanageable by democratic methods.

In supreme crises the dilemma is presented absolutely. Possibly a war can be fought for democracy; it cannot be fought democratically. Possibly a sudden revolution may be made to advance democracy; but the revolution itself will be conducted by a dictatorship. Democracy may be defended against its enemies but it will be defended by a committee of safety. The history of the wars and revolutions since 1914 is ample evidence on this point. In the presence of danger, where swift and concerted action is required, the methods of democracy cannot be employed.

That is understandable enough. But how is it that the democratic method should be abandoned so commonly in more leisurely and less catastrophic times? Why in time of peace should people provoke that centralization of power which deprives them of control over the use of that power? Is it not a probable answer to say that in the presence of certain issues, even in time of peace, the dangers have seemed sufficiently menacing to cause people to seek remedies, regardless of method, by the shortest and easiest way at hand?

It could be demonstrated, I think, that the issues which have seemed so overwhelming were of two kinds: those which turned on the national defense or the public safety and those which turned on the power of modern capitalism. Where the relations of a people to armed enemies are in question or where the relations of employee, customer or farmer to large industry are in question the need for solutions has outweighed all interest in the democratic method.

In the issues engendered by the rise of the national state and the development of large scale industries are to be found the essentially new problems of the modern world. For the solution of these problems there are few precedents. There is no established body of custom and law. The field of international affairs and the field of industrial relations are the two great centers of anarchy in society. It is a pervasive anarchy. Out of the national state with its terrifying military force, and out of great industry with all its elaborate economic compulsion, the threat against personal security always rises. To offset it somehow, to check it and thwart it, seemed more important than any finical regard for the principle of assent.

And so to meet the menace of the national state, its neighbors sought to form themselves into more powerful national states; to tame the power of capitalism they supported the growth of vast bureaucracies. Against powers that were dangerous and uncontrolled they set up powers, nominally their own, which were just as vast and just as uncontrolled.

3

But only for precarious intervals has security been attained by these vast balances of

power. From 1870 to 1914 the world was
held in equilibrium. It was upset, and the
world has not yet found a new order. The
balances of power within the nations are no
less unsteady. For neither in industry
nor in international affairs has it yet been
possible to hold any balance long enough
to fix it by rule and give it an institutional
form. Power has been checked by power
here and there and now and then but
power has not been adjusted to power and
the terms of the adjustment settled and
accepted.

The attempt to bring power under control
by offsetting it with power was sound enough
in intention. The conflicting purposes of
men cannot be held under pacific control
unless the tendency of all power to become
arbitrary is checked by other force. All the
machinery of conference, of peaceful negotiation, of law and the rule of reason is workable
in large affairs only where the power of the
negotiators is neutralized one against the

other. It may be neutralized because the parties are in fact equally powerful. It may be neutralized because the weaker has invisible allies among the other powers of the world, or in domestic affairs among other interests in society. But before there can be law there must be order, and an order is an arrangement of power.

The worst that can be said of the nationalists and collectivists is that they attempted to establish balances of power which could not endure. The pluralist at least would say that the end they sought must be attained differently, that in place of vast wholesale balances of power it is necessary to create many detailed balances of power. The people as a whole supporting a centralized government cannot tame capitalism as a whole. For the powers which are summed up in the term capitalism are many. They bear separately upon different groups of people. The nation as a unit does not encounter them all, and cannot deal with them all. It is to the different groups of people concerned that we must look for the power which shall offset the arbitrary power that bears upon them. The reduction of capitalism to workable law is no matter of striking at it wholesale by general enactments. It is a matter of defeating its arbitrary power in detail, in every factory, in every office, in every market, and of turning the whole network of relations under which industry operates from the dominion of arbitrary forces into those of settled rules.

And so it is in the anarchy among nations. If all the acts of a citizen are to be treated as organically the actions of that nation, a stable balance of power is impossible. Here also it is necessary to break down the fiction of identity, to insist that the quarrel of one business man with another is their quarrel, and not the nation's, a quarrel in which each is entitled to a vindication of his right to fair adjudication but not to patriotic advocacy of his cause. It is only by this dis-

sociation of private interests that the mass
of disputes across frontiers can gradually be
brought under an orderly process. For a
large part, perhaps the greatest part, of the
disputes between nations is an accumulated
mass of undetermined disputes between their
nationals. If these essentially private disputes could be handled, without patriotic
fervor and without confusing an oil pros-
pector with the nation as a whole, with governments acting as friends of the court and not
as advocates for a client, the balance of power
between governments would be easier to
maintain. It would not be subject to constant assault from within each nation by
an everlasting propaganda of suspicion by
private interests seeking national support.
And if only the balance of power between
governments could be stabilized long enough
to establish a line of precedents for international conference, a longer peace might
result.

4

These in roughest outline are some of the
conclusions, as they appear to me, of the
attempt to bring the theory of democracy
into somewhat truer alignment with the
nature of public opinion. I have conceived
public opinion to be, not the voice of God,
nor the voice of society, but the voice of the
interested spectators of action. I have, therefore, supposed that the opinions of the spectators must be essentially different from those
of the actors, and that the kind of action they
were capable of taking was essentially different too. It has seemed to me that the public
had a function and must have methods of its
own in controversies, qualitatively different
from those of the executive men; that it was
a dangerous confusion to believe that private
purposes were a mere emanation of some
common purpose.

This conception of society seems to me
truer and more workable than that which

endows public opinion with pantheistic powers. It does not assume that men in action have universal purposes; they are denied the fraudulent support of the fiction that they are the agents of a common purpose. They are regarded as the agents of special purposes, without pretense and without embarrassment. They must live in a world with men who have other special purposes. The adjustments which must be made are society, and the best society is the one in which men have purposes which they can realize with the least frustration. When men take a position in respect to the purposes of others they are acting as a public. And the end of their acting in this rôle is to promote the conditions under which special purposes can be composed.

It is a theory which puts its trust chiefly in the individuals directly concerned. They initiate, they administer, they settle. It would subject them to the least possible interference from ignorant and meddlesome outsiders, for in this theory the public intervenes only when there is a crisis of maladjustment, and then not to deal with the substance of the problem but to neutralize the arbitrary force which prevents adjustment. It is a theory which economizes the attention of men as members of the public, and asks them to do as little as possible in matters where they can do nothing very well. It confines the effort of men, when they are a public, to a part they might fulfill, to a part which corresponds to their own greatest interest in any social disturbance; that is, to an intervention which may help to allay the disturbance, and thus allow them to return to their own affairs.

For it is the pursuit of their special affairs that they are most interested in. It is by the private labors of individuals that life is enhanced. I set no great store on what can be done by public opinion and the action of masses.

5

I have no legislative program to offer, no new institutions to propose. There are, I believe, immense confusions in the current theory of democracy which frustrate and pervert its action. I have attacked certain of the confusions with no conviction except that a false philosophy tends to stereotype thought against the lessons of experience. I do not know what the lessons will be when we have learned to think of public opinion as it is, and not as the fictitious power we have assumed it to be. It is enough if with Bentham we know that "the perplexity of ambiguous discourse . . . distracts and eludes the apprehension, stimulates and inflames the passions."

INDEX

191